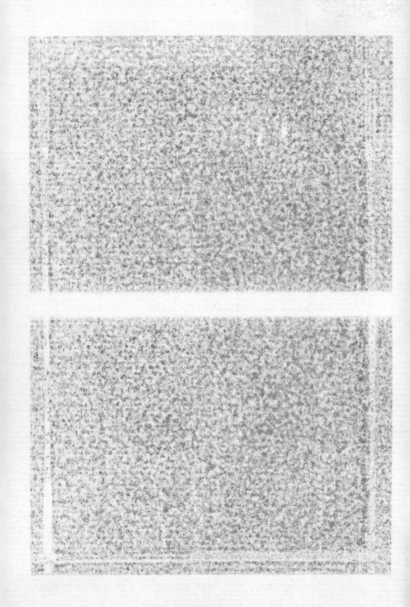

ENGLISH RECUSANT LITERATURE
1558–1640

Selected and Edited by
D. M. ROGERS

Volume 386

JOHANN VON TRITHEIM
A Three-fold Mirrour
1633

JOHANN VON TRITHEIM

*A Three-fold Mirrour of
Mans Vanitie and Miserie*
1633

The Scolar Press
1978

ISBN 0 85967 505 X

*Published and printed in Great Britain by
The Scolar Press Limited, 59-61 East Parade,
Ilkley, Yorkshire and
39 Great Russell Street,
London WC1*

NOTE

Reproduced (original size) from a copy in the Bodleian Library, by permission of the Curators. This copy lacks the title-page, which is reproduced in the facsimile from a copy in the Folger Shakespeare Library, by permission of the Trustees.
Reference: Allison and Rogers 830; not in STC.

A THREE-FOLD MIRROVR OF MAN'S VANITIE AND MISERIE.

THE FIRST·VVRITTEN by that learned and Religious Father, IOHN TRITHEMIVS *Monke of the holy Order of S.* BENET, *and Abbot of Spanhem.*

THE TWO OTHERS BY CATHOLICKE Authors vnknowen: Faithfully Englished by the R. FATHER ANTONIE BATT, Monke of the holy Order aforesaid, of the Congregation of England.

Printed at Doway by LAVRENCE KELLAM, at the signe of the holy Lambe, 1633.

TO Mᵣ. NOBLE AND

VERTVOVS PATRONESSE

MAISTRESSE

ANNE ARONDELLE

THE ELDER.

OF CHEDIOKE.

O *whome could I more*
fitlie addreſſe this three-
fold Mirrour or looking
glaſſe of the worldes va-
nitie and miſerie, then to
your vertuous ſelfe: who haue by long
continuance and conſtant profeſſion of
God's ſeruice planted moſt perfectlie in
your heart a true contempt of the world?
The excellent families both of the Ier-
ninghams, of which you deſcend, and of
the Arondelles, into which by honourable
mariage you are inſerted (noble in the

ā 2 *World,*

world, but more noble in preferring God's
glorie before worrldy immundite) haue
both of them a contentment to see their
virtues and deuotion so happily conioyned
in your soule.

VVhich that it may be alwayes flow-
rishing in grace, and charitie, and true
deuotion, some little inductiue may be this
small labour of mine; little worth indee
for what is mine owne in it (which is onely the translation) but verie much to be
prized, considering the learned Authors,
and the heauenly truth, contained therein.
And what I intended by this labour, that
I purpose to foreward by my daily prayers;
I meane the happie consummation of your
soule in all goodnes and glorie, as being
obliged to this dutifull respect for many
titles, which tie me to remaine, as I haue
alwayes beene.

Your dutifull Beadsman.

BR. ANTONIE BATT.

Approbatio Ordinarij.

Hic liber, cui titulus, Speculum triplex humanæ miseriæ, *à* R. P. ANTONIO BATTO *Ordinis* S. *Benedicti, ex Joanne Trithemio & alijs pijs Authoribus concinnatus, dignus est, qui à Catholicis legatur; nihil habens fidei aut moribus contrarium. Actum Duaci* 15. *Julij, Anno* 1633.

GEORGIVS COLVENERIVS
S. Theol. Doct. & eiusdem
Regius Ord. Prof. Collegiat·
Ecclesiæ. S. Petri Præpositus
Duac. Acad. Cancellarius,
& librorum Censor.

Licentia & Approbatio Præsat.

Nos Fr. Sigebertus Bagshaw, Congregarionis Anglicanæ Ordinis S. Benedicti Presbyter & Monachus, eiusdemque Congregationis Præses generalis, per præsentes facultatem concedimus R. P. Antonio, dictæ Congregationis nostræ Secretario, committendi prelo quædam opuscula deuota, ex Ioanne Trithemio, alijsq; pijs Authoribus decerpta, & a dicto Patre in idioma Anglicum traducta. In cuius rei fidem his subscripsimus, sigillumq; nostrum apposuimus, die 11. Iulij, anno Domini 1633.

Locus * sigilli

Fr. Sigibertus Bagshaw
Præses, qui supra.

A

TABLE OF THE FIRST
Mirrour of man's vanitie and miserie.

VIII.

F I N I S.

A SHORT TREATISE,

WRITTEN BY THAT MOST LEARNED AND Religious Father,

IOHN TRITHEMIVS,

MONKE OF THE HOLY ORDER OF S. BENET, AND Abbot of Spanhem; concerning the vanitie and miserie of the life of man.

CHAPTER I.

An exhortation to a sinnefull soule, not to deferre the amendement of her life.

 I THENCE this present life is in a manner nothing, if it be compared to that celestiall happines, after which we sigh so often; I cannot sufficientl

A   admir

admire thy madnes, ô my foule; for
that this place of feiourning (which
thou oughreft to bewayle, feeing it is
prolonged) thou endureft so conten-
tedly, as if it were thy cou.trie and
true place of abode. It is a thing, I fay,
worthy of admiration, yet arguing
thy folishnes and indifcretion: that
fetting afide the dainties of eternal
beatitude, thou doft fo greedily feede
vpon the huskes of this wretched and
bewitching world. O fenfleffe foole:
who forgetting thy fathers goodnes fo
gratious and liberall, doft follow after
things that are fickle and fraile, being
vnmindfull of thofe that are eternal.
Thou feekeft heere in a place of pilgrimage after vaine comfort and confolation, who art inuited to a kingdome. But thou art deceiued, ô my
foule; in this life there is no countrie:
it is onely the way, by which we walke
towards felicitie. For the holy Apoftle

Heb.13. doth affirme: *We haue not heere a permanent citie: but We feeke that, Which is to
come.* Howbeit that heauenly citie ad-
mitteth none, but fuch as are enamou-
red of the fame. If thou doft defire it,

why

why doft thou not haften towards it?
The heate of chaitie knoweth no delay.

We are placed in this life to gaine
our expenses by holy exercises to carrie vs to life euerlafting : where he,
that is carelefle now in time of fowing,
shall neuer reape corne. Where loue is,
there is poffeffion. Loue that therefore, which thou maieft not loofe :
feeke that which thou maieft lawfully
euerlaftingly poffeffe. Behold the
world paffeth away, and the concupifcence thereof : neither wilt thou e-
uer be permitted to returne againe to
this life. Wherefore thou oughteft to
be verie warie, leaft thou perifh with
the world, that thus paffeth away : becaufe if thou loue the world that is
tranfitorie and fleeting, doubtleffe
thou wilt runne with the fame to deftruction.

Now then (ô finnefull foule) turne
into thy reft. Returne, ô defolate
daughter, to the guide of thy youth.
Haue recourfe ô wandering sheepe,
to thy Creator. *What is the matter, that* Baruc
thou art in the land of thine enemies? *Thou* 3.

A 2   **art**

art waxen old in a strange land, thou art defiled with the dead: thou art reputed with them, that goe downe into hell. And why soe? Because thou hast forsaken the fountaine of wisdome: thou hast departed from God by walking the vnknowne pathes of disobediéce and rebellion; thou hast violated thy first faith of baptisme. For if thou hadst, walked in the way of God, if thou hadst resisted the vitious passions of thy flesh, thou hadst doubtlesse dwelt vpon earth in peace. *But learne where*

Ibidem.   *wisdome is, where strength is, where vnderstanding is: that thou maist know withall where is the long continuance of life and liuing, where the light of the eies, and peace is.* But he that hath fallen, let him adde to rise againe. Why then dost thou delay? Why dost thou deferre the necessarie amendement of thy life? For the

Eccl.5.   scripture saith: *Slacke not to be conuerted to our Lord, and deferre not from day to day.* Because he that is indisposed to begin to do well to day, will be more vnapt to morrow. Why therefore dost thou place this dayes saluatió, in to morrow which is doubtfull and vncertaine?

Doe

Doe good, leaft it repent thee to late,
attend to thy fpirituall gaine: for death
will come fooner then thou doft imagin. Now therefore, ô wretched foule,
what other courfe doth remaine , but
to giue thy felfe to teares and lamentation : to bewaile thy life paft. and to
liue better in time to come ? O miferable condition of mans life : which
doth not grieue afmuch as it knoweth
it felfe: but rather reioyceth as fecure,
for afmuch as it knoweth not it felfe.
O alwayes hurtfull fecuritie of the
foule, which neglecteth vertue, nou-
rifheth vice, and shamefully confu-
meth the wholefome time allotted for
penance. How long wilt thou remaine
thus fluggish, ô my foule ? how long
wilt thou diffemble ? Thou art altogether growne old in finne , and durft
thou prefume, as if thou hadft the fecuritie of holy men ? What are thy
fruits, ô vnfruitfull tree ? What good
works haft thou produced? Verily thou
art an vnprofitable branch, worthy to
be burned. Thou art fruitleffe and bar-
ren : neither is thy fruit any other, but
the pricking thornes of finne: which

I would

I would to God did so prick, as to
moue thee to comp unction: and were
so bitter, as to be abolished out of thy
mind. O withered wood, void of all
good fruit: to what end dost thou oc-
cupie the ground?

O my soule, thou art an vnfruitfull
tree, which that supreme housholder
God almightie hath for a long time
Luc. 13. permitted to remaine in his vineyard
without bearing fruit; which he hath
watered with the dew of his diuine
graces, and dunged with manifold
guifts and fauours. Beware therefore,
least in the end thou appeare to be bar-
ren: least thou deferre thy good purposes of doing penance ouer long, and
so loose this acceptable time. For the
vniuersal iudge, who now so patiently
endureth thee in hope of amendemét,
will more grieuously damne thee in
the end, if thou amend not. Consider
how thou wilt be able to meete him,
who commeth to take an accompt of
thy whole life and actions. What answere wilt thou make thé, ô my soule:
who art now defiled with so many sinnes? What, I say, wilt thou then replie?

                                        To

To hide thy selfe will be impossible, sithence thou wilt be summoned to appeare before him, that knoweth all. To appeare likewise will be a thing verie dreadfull, vnlesse to the good; who in this life do patiently suffer miseries and iniuries for the loue of God: who loue the ioyes of eternal beatitude, who loath the delightes of this wretched world. There all things are apparantly knowne, there the thoughtes of men's hearts lie open, there no sinne (be it neuer to secret) can remaine hidden. Manie sinnes will then rush out on a sodaine (as it were out of ambush) which now are esteemed either none, or verie trifles.

Happie is that soule, which by carefull meditation preuenteth this day of reuenge; which now remaining in flesh, conuerteth her selfe to holy exercises: and with all care and diligence keepeth cleane the house of her conscience. No mā well be able to appeare confidently in the presence of that internal iudge, who doth not keepe himselfe pure and innocēt from
this

this wicked world. For euerie one that
remembreth that he hath offended his
Lord and iudge, feareth to come to his
iudgement. Becauſe by how much the
more he knoweth himſelfe to be guiltie , by ſo much the more he refuſeth
to appeare before ſo great a maieſtie.
Howbeit he ſtriueth in vaine to flie
from the preſence of that iudge , who
filleth all things with his preſence.
And verily to wicked men to appeare
then before that ſupreme iudge will
be a thing intolerable: contrarily to lie
hidden will be altogither impoſſible.
For the holy Apoſtle ſaieth : *We ſhall all
ſtand before the iudgement ſeate of Chriſt:
that euerie one may receiue the reward of his
Worke.*

Rom.14

There the iuſt man ſhall ſtand in
great confidence before our Lord, re-
ceiuing the recompence of his appro-
ued faith : for that he hath behaued
himſelfe in this life as a ſtranger to the
world: for that liuing in fleſh he hath
manfully ſubdued the vices of the
fleſh, and with his whole heart ſighed
after coleſtiall happines. Contrariwiſe
they that liuing in fleſh do now haue
this

this life as their countrie, who gape after honours, and thirst after riches, the
one being vaine, the other transitorie:
who ouerwhelme themselues in the
mud and sinke of sinne; shall stand
there before the tribunal seate of
Christ, their confidence being changed into shame and confusion.

O who is wise, and will vnderstand
these things? Who is prudent, and will
be prudently affraid? That vnderstanding future dangers he may feare, and
fearing, may escape them by care? As
long as we liue in this mortal life, we
are in the way to heauen: in which
we are not permitted to stand still by
slouth and lasinesse, but are commanded to goe forward from vertue to
vertue, sighing after the repose of eternal happines. In this way he fainteth,
that goeth not foreward: and he that
doth not runne, goeth backward. For
no man (as I haue alreadie said) can
stand still, so long as he liueth in this
world. Howbeit our going forward in
our way, is to goe forward in vertue:
to goe backward, is to grow negligent
in doing good. Then we truly tend to-

B   wards

wards our heauenly countrie, when
we obey the commaundemēts of God
and of his Church with a religious sin-
ceritie.

Whosoeuer therfore desireth to attaine to that celestial mansion: let him
in the way seeke no delay, or comfort
of distraction. For it is apparant that
he doth not loue his countrie as he
should, that is delighted with the beau
tie of his banishments. He therefore
can neuer attaine to that heauenly
paradise, that doth not despise all earthly pleasures and contentmēt. They
therefore that desire to goe foreward
in the way of God, must first af all con-
tēne the pleasures of the world, without which true charitie can neuer be
obtained. For Christ (who is charitie it
selfe) hath said : *If any man will come af-*
Mat. 16. *ter me , let him denie himselfe , and take vp*
his crosse , and follow me. This our Lord
Iesus Christ (being the way, the truth,
and the life) hath commāded, taught,
and performed. Christ is the way to
life euerlasting , as he himselfe doth
Io. 14. affirme: † *I am the Way, the truth, and the*
Io. 10. *life:† I am the dore:because no man commeth*
                                    to the

to the father, but by me. Why dost thou
seeke any thing els, ô wretched soule,
why dost thou seeke any thing els? Iesus
Christ being God and man, hath giuen
thee a forme of liuing : who by his
wordes hath taught the contempt of
all things temporal, and confirmed the
same by his example.

Behold God the supreme Vmpire
enuiteth thee to the contempt of the
world, and dost thou make semblance,
as if thou heardst him not ? Why dost
thou not voluntarily forsake the world
for the loue of God almightie , which
of necessitie thou must shortly leaue
by the death of thy bodie? Nothing
vnder the sunne remaineth still at a
stay: but all things as smoke sodainely
vanish away.

CHAPTER II.

*That all wordly things are subiect
to vanitie.*

Vanitie of vanities (said whilome that
most wise preacher) Vanitie of vanities, Eccl. 1.

nities, and all things vanitie. What all things? What vanitie of vanities? All things which with time and alteration passe away, and come to nothing. The world passeth away, and the concupiscence thereof: *and we all die: and as Waters that returne not, We fall do Wne on the earth.* Whatsoeuer therefore doth corrupt and perish, may truly be termed vanitie of vanities. Howbeit all worldly things are subiect to corruption; and consequently all things are vaine, and vanitie of vanities. In hebrew it is *Habal habalim*, which besides the Septuaginta or seuentie Interpreters all haue likewise interpreted it in Grecke, *Atmos atmō*: which we may call a vapour of smoke or thinne ayre, which is quickly dissolued. Now what is so thinne as man, who liueth to day, and to morrow appeareth not? If man be not vanitie, where are all our progenitors? Where are those men that whilome were so famous in their generations, who haue subdued many peoples and kingdomes? Where is old Mathusalem? Where is that most potēt tirant Nemrod? Where is that most strong Sampson?

1. King.
17.

son? Where is that most faire Abſolon?
Where is that most wiſe Salomon?
Where is Cræſus now that abounded in
gold. Where is Alexander the great,
the conquerour of the world? Where
is Plato that arch-philoſopher? Where is
that prince of Poets Homer? Where is
now the whole rable rout of Philoſo-
phers and Poets? All for many yeares
ſince haue died and paſt away, and
(which is worſt of all) haue perished
in their vanitie. What doth all their
former power now profit them? what
do their honoures, riches, and fame
now auaile them? Behold they now
ſleepe in the duſt: and are cleane forgotten, as if they had neuer beene.
Whatſoeuer therefore is in the world,
is vaine: man is vaine: riches are vaine
honoures are vaine † For the things
that are ſeene, are temporall: but thoſe things
that are not ſeene, eternal. For the holy
Apoſtle ſaieth: † The creature is made
ſubiect to vanitie, not willing, but for him,
that made it ſubiect in hope: becauſe the creature alſo it ſelfe ſhall be deliuered from the
ſeruitude of corruption, into the libertie of
the children of God.

2.Cor. 4

Rom. 8.

So long

So long all things are vaine, vntill
that come which is perfect. All things
therefo e are vaine, that are contained
vnder the cope of heauen. No temporall thing doth remaine : no earthly
thing doth continue conſtant and
firme : no mortal thing doth laſt long.
What if thou be a great prince, and liue
many yeares vpon earth ? Perchance
thou maieſt deferre death for a while:
but wholy to eſcape death is a thing
impoſſible. A day will creepe vpon
thee, eare thou be aware of, and will
bereaue thee of all thy hope and life.
To day thou art a Prince, to day thou
art a Lord, and mightie in the world:
to morrow thou wilt be dead, and thy
carion carcaſe will be hidden vnder
ground. Behold an Emperour, who
yeſterday was great, is to day carried
to his graue to be wormes meat : and
he that yeſterday was clothed in purple and cloth of gold, and other braue
attire; is to day (in a manner ſtarke
naked) throwne into his ſepulcher.
Yeſterday he ruled ouer peoples and
nations: to day he hath loſt his life and
empire, being neuer to returne to the
ſame

fame any more. Yefterday when he
paffed by, euerie one bowed the knee
vnto him: to day he is carried dead to
his graue, and no man doth vouchfafe
afmuch as to moue his cappe vnto him.
Yefterday men were conftrained to
ftoupe vnto him: to day being dead,
he is tormented in hell, neither is any
man able to deliuer him. Yefterday
when he fpake, euerie one kept filence
and liftned vnto him: to day he crieth
out in torments, and no man pitieth
him. Yefterday, as if he should haue
liued for euer, he abounded with daintie cheere: to day through the heate of
hell fire, he is verie thirftie, and no
man giueth him fo much as a cup of
cold water. Yefterday fitting as a
iudge, fhing with gold and pretious
ftones, he drew the eies of the beholders to admire his greatnes: to day
being wrapt vp in a poore winding
sheete, he becommeth full of filthy
thy wormes. Yefterday he was delighted with the fweet melodie of
mufitians: to day being in hell, he is
deluded with the mocks and fcoffs of
the diuells. Yefterday his fatte and dilicate

licate bodie was cherished with the
chonest bathes that humane art could
imagin: to day he is tormented in hell
with fire and brimstone; euen as it is
written: *As much as shee hath glorified
her selfe, and hath beene in delicacies: so
much giue her torment and mourning.* And
againe: *The mightie shall mightily suffer
torments.* What good then will the honours, riches, or dignities of former
times, doe vnto the wretched soule?
There the impious haue ceased from
tumult: there the honour of earthly
power is contemned: there the greatnes of riches is despised. Why therefore
ô insolēt power dost thou grow proud?
Why, ô insatiable glouttonie of gold,
dost thou looke bigge? Whatsoeuer
honour or riches thou dost possesse in
the world, thou wilt looie full quickly,
and perchance this may happē to day.
And when thou shalt passe to hell ouer
that infernall floud of Acheron, thou
shalt carrie nothing at all out of this
world with thee, sauing the good and
and bad deedes onely, which thou
hast committed in thy mortal bodie.

*The World passeth and the concupiscence
thereof:*

Apoc.
18.

wis 6.

1.Io.2.

thereof: all earthly power paſſeth away on a ſodaine;neither is there any thing of long continuance vnder the ſunne. What auaileth it , if a man be great vpon earth; if he be potent,ſtrong,faire, rich, or learned ? The life of all men is moſt ſhort: neither is there diſtinction of perſons or dignities : whatſoeuer is mortal, dieth. For the wiſe mã ſaieth: *There is no man that may liue alwayes: and* Eccli. 9. *can haue confidence of this thing* . It is appointed to all men to die once:neither can we eſcape death , although we deferre the ſame for many yeares. All things that are framed of earth , returne into earth : the ſpirit being ſet free from the priſon of the fleſh , is haled with violence to the tribunal ſeat of Chriſt , there to receiue according to her works.

Now therefore ò man, how long wilt thou thus ſleepe and ſnort ? how long wilt thou abuſe Gods patience, and mercie , expecting thine amendement ? Why doſt thou not amend thy life ? Behold men die daily before thine eies : children and old

C   men

men depart vnawares: learned and vn-
learned are carried to their graues: and
yet thou thinkeft not of death, but re-
maineft as one altogether careleffe. Be
hold the world runneth to ruine; men
perish, cities and rownes are ouerthrowne, nothing vnder the funne
doth continue long: and yet notwith-
ftanding thy hard heart is not moued
to compunction. Death commeth
ftealing on, thine end is neerer then
thou doft imagin.

Why doft thou delay? Why doft thou
expect? Why doft thou linger? Why
doft thou not doe penance wretched
man, whilft thou art healthy and
ftrong? Behold the world paffeth, and
thou followeft him: he deceiueth and
thou loueft him: he lieth, and thou re-
lieft on him. Thou perisheft with him
perishing: thou falleft with him fal-
ling: thou art deceiued with him de-
ceiuing. Woe be to the louers of the
world. They are foolish, they are wretched, they are vnfortunate. For verily
whiles they feeke to hold the world as
is were by force: they loofe both heauen and earth at once. They earneftly
                              feeke

seeke after woildly riches and honours, and yet hope to attaine to celestial happines. But our Lord in the
Gospell saieth otherwise. No man, saieth
he, can serue two maisters. Who are those *Mat.6.*
two maisters? God and the world. For
he that loueth God, contemneth the
world. And he that loueth the world,
neglecteth God. You cannot saieth he,
serue God and mammon, that is riches.

This present life is not permanent,
but passeth : it endureth not, but vani-
sheth: it standeth not still at a stay, but
perisheth. It is therefore the way to
our countrie, by which we passe euerie
moment, being no more to returne
into this world. Wherefore he sheweth
himselfe to be but a foolish trauailer,
who gazing on the gay shewes that
are in the way, forgetteth so noble a
countrie: who neglecting things eternal, affecteth those that are vaine and
temporal: and embraseth the world
which is continually readie to fail. For
nothing is more fickle then worldly
fortune : nothing more fraile then the
life of man : nothing more short then
earthly power and dominion.

That

That man therefore is happie, that knoweth how to contemne all things transitorie: who knoweth how to vanquish carnal pleasures; who is able to despise all earthly riches. For all earthly things, that a man possesseth, leaue him alone at the hower of his death: in so much that he that was rich, and had many things in his possession; when he dieth, carrieth nothing with him. Heerevpon the wise man crieth out,

Eccle.1. saying. *What hath a man more of all his labour, Whereby he laboureth vnder the sunne?* Behold how many do now sweat in the labour of this world; they watch night and day by heaping together riches, they traine vp their children, and build high houses: and in the middest of their worke they perish; and carrie nothing at all with them, but returne stark naked into the earth, frō whence they had their beginning.

Eccle.1. *A generation passeth, and a generation cometh; but the earth standeth for euer.* Some dying, others are borne : and whilst generation succedeth to generation, nothing in the world remaineth constāt and firme. What is more

vaine

vaine then this vanitie? The earth remaineth firme, which was made for
man: and man himfelfe being Lord of
the earth, is fodainely turned into
duſt. There is no memorie of thoſe firſt
inhabitants of the world, that haue
gone before vs: and like as oblivion
doth hide thoſe things from vs, which
are paſt: ſo our poſteritie will not
know thoſe things, which either are
done now, or ſhall be heere after: and
all things will paſſe away in ſilence,
and will be hidden, as if they had neuer beene.

All things therefore are vaine: and
not onely vaine, but alſo vanitie of vanities. The world is vaine: becauſe
thoſe followers thereof, whome whiles
they liue, it fauoureth and flattereth; it
faueth not at the hower of their death.
All worldly honours are vaine: becauſe
thoſe whome they make great before
men, they fodainely at the hower of
death leaue alone, depriued of all honour and reputation. Riches are vaine:
becauſe they do not deliuer their poſ-
feſſors from death, but do damn them
more deeper by abuſing them. All
earthly

earthly power is vaine: becaufe thofe whome it hath raifed to the height of preferment, it forfaketh, and throweth downe head-long to hell in a moment. Nobilitie and gentrie is vaine: becaufe thofe that before men it maketh glorious and great, it permitteth after death to become wormes meat. To be borne of rich parentage is alfo vaine: becaufe he that is feparated from others aflong as he ftaieth in the world by his noble parētage, is compared being dead to beafts that perish. Carnal kinred likewife is nothing worth, for that it cannot hinder the fentence of death. The fweet knot of wedlock is vaine: becaufe thofe that it loueth whilft they liue, it immediatly leaueth affoone as they are dead. The laborious education of children, (not without great coft and charges) is vaine: becaufe the parents whome it loue:h being aliue, it detefteth being dead. Whatfoeuer feemeth pretious in the world is vaine: becaufe it is loft on a fodaine.

Sithence

Sithence therefore all earthly things are vaine; it followeth, that whosoeuer loueth vanitie, desireth (as one that is vaine) to vanish away to nothing. Hence the blessed Apostle S. Iohn admonisheth vs, saying: *Little children, loue not the World, nor those things that are in the World. If any man loue the World, the charitie of the Father is not in him. Because all that is in the World, is the concupiscence of the flesh, and the concupiscence of the eies, and the pride of life, Which is not of the Father, but is of the World.* Wherefore we ought to flie the world, as the chiefe enemie of our saluation: because it euilly rewardeth those that follow the same, sending them headlong to eternall damnation.

1. Ioan. 2.

CHAP.

CHAPTER III.

That this prefent life is a certaine pilgrimage from our heauenly countrie.

2.Cor.
5.

Iob.7.

THe holy Apoftle faieth : *As long as we are in the bodie, we are pilgrimes from our Lord* : And bleffed Iob auoucheth in like manner ; *That the life of man vpon earth is a Warre-fare.* If therefore we be pilgrimes, why do we not haften towards our countrie: if we be fouldiers why do we not wage warre?

Behold we know that during the time of this life we are pilgrimes, and yet we do not pray that our banifhment may be ended, but forgetting our heauenly countrie, we loue the prifon of our pilgrimage. He that is a bad fouldier, feareth the end of the warre: fo euerie one that aboundeth with riches and honoures, feareth death.

death. For if he had fought valiantly,
he would haften to receiue his pay.
But becaufe he knoweth, that he hath
committed many outrages, he is exceedingly affraid to iffue forth of
the bodie, and to appeare before
the fupreme iudge. And why doft
thou not then prepare thy felfe
(wretched man) to meete thy Sauiour at his comming? Why doft thou
not doe penance whiles thou art healthy and ftrong? He dieth fecurely, that
liueth vertuoufly. Know that thou art
but a pilgrime vpon earth, and therefore let thy conuerfation be fuch, as
thou wouldft defire it should be at the
hower of thy death. Why doft thou deferre thy good purpoles from day to
day? Why doft thou not begin that to
day, which thou doft put ouer vntill
to morrow?

The hope of longer life hath deceiued many: becaufe aflong as they defire to liue longer in the world, they
shamefully let paffe the time of repê-
tance. For oftentimes when a man
doth procraftinate the will of his conuerfion: being preuented by death by

D   the

the iuſt iudgement of God, he looſeth both will and meanes to amend. For God almightie, who hath promiſed pardon to thoſe that are penitét, hath not promiſed to morrow, to thoſe that are negligent. Heerevpon the holy ſcripture warneth vs, ſaying : To day if you will heare his voyce, harden not your hearts. God alwaies crieth to day, he alwaies admoniſheth vs to day, and we expeſt till to morrow. The laſt day of our life will ſhortly come, when we ſhall pray to haue the time of penáce prolonged, and ſhall not obtaine the ſame. We now negleſt to doe penance being ſound and ſtrong : at the hower of our death we promiſe great amédment, when we are able to doe iuſt nothing. Why do we not doe that now, which then we ſhall wiſh to haue done?

The reward of our labour is to be expeſted at the end, not new labours to be vndertaken. For. as I haue ſaid alreadie, this preſent life is nothing els, but a pilgrinage and certaine paſſage to our countrie: in which we cannot long ſtand ſtill at a ſtay, but of neceſſitie

Pſal. 94

cessitie must alwaies goe forewards in
our iourney. Each hower of time doth
diminish part of our life : and euerie
minute doth cut off somewhat of our
pilgrimage. He then that desireth to
goe readily to his heauenly countrie,
let him lay aside all solicitude of things
transitorie. For the way to heauen is
narrow : it receiueth not him that is
loaden with riches : it despiseth him
that is puffed vp with honours : it ad-
mitteth not him that is apt to fall
through vice. It *is easier* (saieth our Mat.19.
Lord) For *a camell to passe through the eie
of a needle, then for a rich man to enter into
the kingdome of heauen.*

Wherefore if riches abound, place
not thy heart vpon them : doe not co-
uetously possesse them : do not ouer
carefully keepe them. *Better is a little to*   Psal. 39.
the iust, aboue much riches of sinners. Heerevpon the holy Apostle doth admonish
vs, saying : *hauing food, and wherewith to*   1. Tim.
be couered, with these we are content. For   6.
*they that desire to become rich, fall into
temptation, and the snare of the diuell.* What
good doth your gold and siluer doe
you, ô ye rich worldlings? How long
            D 2   do

do you thirst, and seeke after gold?
What doth your money in your cof-
fers? For whome do you hoard it vp?
For your selues, or for your children?
Not for your selues, because you can
possesse nothing long in this world.
It is for your children therefore that
you heape vp riches, whome you make
inheritors of your couetousnes? But
you that haue no children, for whome
do you take all this paine? for whome
do you collect so much coine? Not for
your selues, but for others: not for
your owne children, but for strangers.
Being in the pilgrimage of this life,
you goe loaden for the loue of others,
with the heauie burden of riches: and
whiles you seeke to enrich your children, you goe astray like fooles from
the way of truth and saluation. At the
hower of death your mids are so troubled with worldly businesses, that you
cannot admit so much as one good
thought concerning heauenly happines. You wholy consume the short
time of your sicknes in disposing your
temporal affaires, and take little care
(God wott) of the saluation of your
                                        soules.

soules. You make your will, and dispose of your things temporall: but of the wounds of your soule you make no accompt at all. You set downe euerie particular that you would haue obserued in the pompe of your funeralls, but in prouiding for your soule, whether it is to goe after death you are altogether carelesse. You take no small paines in making your last will and testament, and yet whether it shall euer be accomplished or no, you know not.

For oftentimes a couetous testatour hath knaues for his notaries. And worthilie. For he that is vnfaithfull to himselfe, how can he expect that an other should be faithfull vnto him? Behold a rich couetous mã, that gaue little or nothíg in almes aslóg as he liued cõmaundeth at his death many guifts to be giuen to the poore, to Monasteries, and churches, and trusteth more to others, then to himselfe.

Howbeit the testatour being dead, we know for the most part what followeth afterward. Sometimes the kindred of the partie departed get the
will

will into their hands : at other times
the secular power opposeth it selfe
with violence : and now and then the
executors catch and snatch all the best
things they can find, and contemne
to accomplish what the testatour cō-
manded. Moreouer if thoſe falſe notaries chance to meete with ſome rare
peece of gold or ſiluer, or which is of
ſome ancient ſtāpe, if they ſee a good
booke, or any thing that doth like
them, they take it away in conuert; or
if they cannot handſomely ſteale it,
they fraudulently and craftily buy it
of their companions. I do not ſay, that
good notaries or ſcriueners will doe
this, but ſuch as are knaues. And it
hapneth verie often, that couetous
perſons are badly dealt withall after
their death: that they that would not
giue almes whiles they were liuing:
should by the iuſt iudgement of God,
be neglected after death, euen by their
owne children and kindred.

A rich and couetous man thinketh
that he shall liue a long time in the
world: and whiles he feareth to diminish his goods in the way, he looſeth
both

both life and goods together. He ac-
coūeth himielfe a citizé of this earthly region, and make h no hafte to that
heauenly kingdome. Howbeit he is
taken away in a moment, and adiudged to hell, there to remaine in perpetual torment. What will the vaine riches of the world then auaile him,
which now hinoer him from attai-
ning heauen? *Their filuer and their gold* Ezech.7
shall not be able to deliuer them in the day
of the furie of our Lord.

O wretched world, how badly doft
thou require thy followers, whome
thou doft fend to be torméted in euerlafting fire. Thou doft oftentimes exalt
thofe that loue thee : and whiles they
truft in temporall commodities, they
fodainly defcend to hell without repentance. *All power is of short life* : and Eccli.
the poffeffion of riches is not ftable 10.
vpon earth. For the life of man is short:
earthly power is shorter : but profperitie in both is shorteft of all.

Confider therefore thy condition ô
man : confider thy life, confider thy
death. Thy condition is mortal and
fubieét to corruption : thy life short:
thy

thy death certaine. Liue so, as that thou
maiest not feare to die. Death is not
terrible to a good conscience: for that
it hopeth thereby to attaine to eternal
happines. If thou be rich and strong,
consider that within a while thou shalt
be poore and infime : becaufe he that
to day is a great Prince, may to morrow be a dead carcasse. Let not the
vaine prosperitie of the world deceiue
thee: let not the desire of gold seduce
thee : let not short honour and pompe
make thee proud. Doe good whiles
Prou.3. thou liueft : *Honour our Lord With thy
substance* : becaufe after death it will no
longer be in thy power. Truft not more to others, then to thy selfe: and
what thou doft desire to haue done after thy death, performe whiles thou
liueft. It argueth no discretion to commit that to be diftributed at thy death,
which thou thy selfe maiest order now
being yet aliue. It is not secure to deferre the doing of that good; which
may be neglected. Know, that thou art
but a pilgrime in this world, and desire not more then is necessarie for the
prouision of thy iournéy.

                                    Doe

Doe good to all men whiles thou
art able: labour as a good souldier of
Iesus Christ, because thy warre-fare
will shortly be at an end. Whatsoeuer
thou shalt doe in the way of this pilgrimage, thou shalt assuredly receiue
at the end of thy voyage. *Whatsoeuer*
therefore thy hand is able to doe, Worke it   Eccle.9.
instantly; because after death there is no
more working, but a reward is giuen
according to what thou hast done. Fly
the desires of the flesh, which fight a-
gainst the soule: flie idlenes. flie vanitie. Thou shalt labour a little now, and
for a verie short time; and for thy
guerdon thou shalt receiue life euerlasting.

Behold death doth hasten: thou
canst not liue long: thou wilt die on a
sodaine. And then whatsoeuer thou
hast scraped together for many yeares
before, thou wilt loose in an hower.
Of all that thou hast, thou wilt carrie
nothing with thee: neither gold, nor
siluer, nor honour, nor power. For all
earthly things will leaue thee in a moment: onely thy coscience will follow
thee with his ornaments. Neither ri-

E   ches,

ches, nor worldly brauerie, nor earthly
vanitie will doe a man any good when
he cometh to die : onely good workes
(if he haue done any) will comefort
the afflicted foule in that extreme miferie.

CHAPTER IIII.

*VVhat courfe of life we ought to
vndertake.*

THE breuitie of this short life doth
admonish vs, not to fpend the
time vnprofitably that is allotted vs to
doe penance. For time paffeth away
and is irreuocable: and the day which
is not fpent well, is both countable
and culpable. For now is the acceptable time, in which we are commanded to doe good without intermiffió:
for which we may purchafe life euerlafting. Loffe of time is hurtfull and
altogether damnable, fithence that
labouring but for a while, we may
merit

merit rest eternal. Euerie man therefore that is desirous of saluation ought to be verie carefull, least he spend the time vnprofitably which is graunted him to doe well. For now is the time of labouring; after death no man can labour, no man (I meane) can merit any more. Wherefore let euerie one now choose that course of life which is most agreable to his state, in which let him not loose time, which ought to be prized at so high a rate.

Howbeit whosoeuer doth resolue to vndergoe some holy course of life or conuersation, let him seriously cōsider the counsell of the wise man, saying : *Sonne comming to the seruice of God, stand in iustice, and in feare, and prepare thy soule to temptation.* For no man is able to perseuere in his good purposes, that is not carefull to preserue patience. Wherevpon the same wise man saieth in an other place : *If thou hold not thy selfe instantly in the feare of our Lord: thy house will quickly be subuerted.* By thy house, he meaneth thy conscience. For it is written of man, *that he neuer continueth in one state.* Now he

Eccl.2.

Eccl.27.

Iob 14.

E 2 vnder-

vndertaketh a better courſe of life with great feruour and deuotion: and after a while growing tepid, he falleth into his former negligences againe. Now his deuotion is ſo great, that he prayeth with teares; and an hower after he is wholy poſſeſſed with ſlouth and negligence.

When feruour of ſpirit is preſent, we promiſe great matters: if we be neuer ſo little tempted, we preſently forget our good purpoſes. Howbeit that reſolution of amendment was neuerfirme, which could be loſt vpon Eccli.27 to ſlight an occaſion. For *a foole is changed as the moone:* but a wiſe man remaineth conſtant in his reſolution. There are many that make ſhew of great deuotion in time of tranquillitie and peace: but aſſone as any temptation doth begin to ariſe, all their deuotion Pſal. 48. doth immediatly periſh. They confeſſe to our Lord, when he doeth good vnto them: but aſſoone as any aduerſitie doth ruſh vpon them, they do not onely caſt aſide their former deuotion, but (which is worſe) they fall to murmuring. And there are ſome, who

when

when they are troubled with any tribulation or aduersitie, pray vnto God verie deuoutly: but assoone as the blast of tribulatiō doth leaue blowing, farewell all deuotion. Againe there are some, who being neither proud in prosperitie, nor dieded in aduersitie, remaine constant in the feare of God: in prosperitie vsing feare, in aduersitie hauing patience for their shield. These onely walke vpright before God: who in all things giuing thanks, dee alwaies in feare build the house of their conscience. Of such as these the wise man saieth: *Blessed is the man, that is alwayes fearefull: but he that is of an obstinate mind, shall fall into euill.* Prou.28

Whosoeuer therefore doth desire to goe forevvard in pietie and godlinesse: whosoeuer doth hasten to eternal happines, let him not depart from the feare of our Lord, and the custodie of himselfe. For if he cast aside for neuer so little a time either the feare of God, or the care of going foreward; if he admit drowsines or melancholy into his mind, he will not long continue constant in those good courses, which

he

he intended. For no negligence is so
little, which doth not encreafe, if it be
conremned. it behoueth him therefore that defireth the faluation of his
foule to put on the armour of patience
and (as much as lieth in his power) to
efchew all negligence: leaft whiles he
confidently thinketh that he goeth
foreward in the way of perfection, he
grow by little and iettle through care-
lefnes to be luke warme.

And fithence a man cannot continue long in one ftate, let him haue a
care to rife againe, although he fall
neuer fo often. A man can neuer attaine to a habit of well doing, vnleffe he
ftudie daylie to renew his affection.
Few there are, that can ftedfaftly fixe
their eies vpõ the funne: but this grace
is onely graunted to them, who (like
eagles) behold Chrift the funne of
iuftice by heauenly contemplation.

Thefe are good and perfect men,
who louing God aboue all things, do
neither feeke nor couet any earthly
thing: Such as thefe neuer withdraw
the eies of their mind from the beames
of the true funne, but onely whé fome
corpo-

corporal neceſſitie doth compell the,
Their eies are alwayes bent vpon that
moſt bright ſunne of iuſtice, becauſe
they inceſſantly lift vp their thoughts
to celeſtial things. But we by reaſon of
our reachleſneſ being like to little
birds, who find our ſelues vnable to
fixe our eies like Eagles on the ſunne
of iuſtice: let vs, Iſay, haue a care fre-
quently to lift vp our eies: to the end
that as often as we turne the ſight of
our mind (by reaſon of ſome corporal
neceſſitie) from the ſpeculation of heauenly things, ſo often we riſe againe
to the contemplation of them.

For no man becometh a Sainct on a
ſodaine ; but we are to mount vp as it
were by certaine ſtepps or degrees to
the height of perfection. Howbeit the
greateſt difficultie of ſpirituall uſe is to
Nouices or beginners in their firſt
onſet : which by little and little is
ouercome by proficients, and wholy
put to flight by ſuch as are perfect. For
neuer any man was able to goe foreward, that begun not in that order as
he ought. Moreouer many begin to
amend their bad liues and conuerſa-
tion,

tion, who neuerthelesse do neuer attaine to perfection : because those faults which to day they seeme to lament with sorrow, they are not affraid to commit againe to morrow. But that resolution of amendement is verie weake and infirme, which is so often broken by a new sinne.

A sinner will arise and he will not: and oftentimes whiles he feareth not to deferre his good purposes, he looseth both opportunitie and possibilitie at once. He tosseth to and fro in the bed of euill custome : which neglecting to infringe, he causeth to himselfe a certaine necessitie of sinning. *For euerie one that committeth sinne, is the seruant of sinne.* Certainely he that by Gods grace might haue stood if he would, before he fell into sinne; is not easily permitted after his fall to arise againe. For the custome of sinne keepeth him downe that is fallen, and without the especial grace of God, permitteth him not to rise againe.

O how many sinners are there at this present, aduiterers, couetous persons, fornicators, vncleane, and such like

Io. 8.

like; who being held captiue by a bad
and long custome, purpose to escape
from the bondage of their ghostly ad-
uersarie, and yet are vnable to free
themselues from his tyránical slauerie.
For euill customes, if they be not resisted, cause a certaine necessitie, which
cannot be auoided. Wherefore it behoueth vs to put our good purposes in
execution with great fortitude and
feruour: because if continual patience
be wanting, the will of mã doth soone
begin to stagger. Let euerie one that is
desirous to goe foreward in his estate,
put on a mind like vnto a rock : not
that I would haue him to gaine-say
good counsel, but that he should manfully resist the temptatiõs of the diuell.
For oftétimes those that thinke themselues most secure, are in greatest danger.

F   CHAP.

CHAPTER V.

*That many and diuerſe things do
withdraw vs from the fruit
of penance.*

NO man is able perfectly to conſider (much leſſe to expreſſe) how
many ſnares, pit-foldes, and impedi-
ments the diuel is wont to expoſe to
entrap thoſe that deſire to doe penāce.
He vſeth a thouſand tricks ād deuices,
that he may recall him from his good
purpoſes, whome he ſeeth to ſeeke
after the remedie of penance. And truly according to the diuerſitie of the
ſtate, ſexe, age, and condition of men,
he inuenteth diuerſe meanes of hur-
ting : and what by himſelfe he cannot
bring to paſſe, he endeauoureth to ac-
compliſh by wicked men by ſondrie
deuices.

And oftentimes he perſecuteth a
penitent man euen vntill death it ſelfe:

and

and whome he permitteth to liue quiet
as a sinner in his wickednes, he endeauoureth to ouerwhelme being conuerted, by infinite tribulations. Sometimes against a man that purposeth to
amend his life he stirreth vp his paul-
trie wife: sometimes he incenseth his
friends and kindesfolke against him:
to the end that whome they ought to
imitate being repentant, they may not
be affraid to reuile and persecute as a
foole and ideot. And if he see, that he
cannot preuaile by this meanes neither, he proceedeth yet further. He
stirreth vp such men as whilome were
his deare companions and friends
vnto hatred: that they which formerly
did delightfully sticke vnto him whiles
he did amisse, may now abandon him
doing penance.

Next the enemie of all goodnes layeth violent hands vpon his temporal
substance: he causeth his house to be
burned: bereaueth him of his honoures, ransacketh his riches: stirreth vp
the magistrates and iudges against
him: soweth dissensions, seeketh occa-
sions. Hoerevpon the secular power

F 2   oppres-

oppresseth the poore innocent: confis-
cateth his goods into the kings exche-
quer, as the goods of a malefactor: and
permitteth him not to liue in quiet.
During these turmoyles the mind of
this poore man, thus estranging himselfe
from the world, is oftentimes verie
grieuously troubled: he feareth that he
is forsaken of God; and vnlesse he put
on the shield of fortitude and patience
against all aduersities that may occurre
he within a while falleth from the holy resolution which he had made of liuing better. But if this champion and
louer of penance fight manfully in all
these things, the combate oftimes
groweth to be more fierce. For when
the diuel seeth that he hath still the
worst, notwithstanding he hath bereaued him of his riches; he bendeth
his forces against the penitents verie
flesh. He inflicteth vpon him by Gods
permission many calamities, that by
impatience he may withdraw him fro
his good purposes.

Sometimes his vnfaithfull wife play-
eth the queane: sometimes shee scol-
deth and reuileth her husband: sometimes

times shee crieth out, that all things
runne to wrack through his negligéce
and default: sometimes shee calleth
him asse and dolt. Why, saith shee, dost
thou consume the whole day in slug-
gish idlenesse? What makest thou so
long in the Church? What hast thou to
doe with such as liue in Monasteries?
how long (a poxe on thee) shall I endure thy hypocrysie? What dost thou
sit muttering alone to thy selfe in thy
chamber? If thou hadst a desire to liue
like a Monke, why didst thou not
enter into a Monasterie? Wretched
woman that I am, whence hath this so
great euill befallen me? I hoped when
I maried thee, to haue found thee a
good husband and thriftie: but contrariwise, thou art not onely negligent
in looking to the affaires of the house,
but likewise dost contemne me as one
that were not worthly to wipe thy shoes.
Hence arise discords and variances
against this poore man that is desirous
to doe penance; hence the wife becometh malitious, hence procedeth the
summa totalis of internal miserie and
distresse.

No

No man can beleeue, except he hath learned it by experience, how great the calamitie of that couple is, that are of contrarie dispositions.

For he that desireth to liue according to the spirit, doth alwaies (for the most part) find his dearest friends to contradict him in it. But if now and then all external tribulation be wanting; yet the diuel doth not thus cease, but be taketh himselfe to inward warres. He suggesteth to the penitent many and sondrie things: he proposeth the difficultie of perseuerance: and craftily sheweth him the frailtie of mans condition. Consequently his inward cogitation saieth: How long shall I endure this rigour of penance?

If he be young and lustie, it will say: Why dost thou foolish felow thus torment thy selfe like a mad man before the time? Thinkest thou that by afflicting thy flesh, thou shalt obtaine the kingdome of God more then others? True it is thou art young and hast strēgth and forces, yet neuerthelesse thou wilt not be able long to endure this labour hour of penance. Tush: rather according to the old saying : Laugh and be merrie , whiles thou art young ; and heereafter when thou art old, then doe penance in Gods name.

But to old men the diuel readeth another lesson : Why thou old dotard (saieth the diuel) dost thou kill thy selfe? Why dost thou not spare thine old age? and why dost thou vtterlie ouerthrow thy weake bodie, by thus mortifying ād afflicting thy selfe vndiscreetly? *God doth not exact robberie in holocaust.* Wherefore follow my counsel, and procede more discreetly. Let thy seruice to God be according to reason, least it be imputed vnto thee as a sinne. God is mercifull , and in lieu of good workes , will accept thy good will. Finally the diuel doth suggest many things to a man that is desirous to doe penance: the flesh likewise vseth many obiectiōs to the same purpose, yea and bringeth many fained reasons, whereby to hinder a man from prosecuting his vertuous resolutions. But a wise and discreet man despiseth all these things : he contemneth all the diuells

sugge-

Esai. 61.

suggestions : he breaketh in peeces all
the worlds bonds by perseuerance.

Such as desire to doe penance are
neuer free from bickerings : such as
flie the world are neuer void of hinderances : becaufe he that is not hit by
the one, is more grieuoufly hurt by the
other. Euerie one feeleth and carrieth
his crofse in himfelfe ; euerie one bea-
reth the burden of his temptations:
for that aslong as we liue in this world,
no mã is exempted frõ being tempted.
And in all thefe things patiéce is need-
full, without which no man is able to
poffeffe his foule Listen not (ô man) to
the suggestions of thy ghostly enemie;
consent not to the fraudulent speeches
of thy bodie; if thou desire to attaine to
eternal felicitie. Omit not to doe penance, whiles thou art young and
strong: for that thou art altogether vncertaine, whether thou shalt liue to be
an old man.

Death openly is at hand, and daily
threatneth to seize vpon old men: and
lieth in waite for such as are young.
For an old man cannot liue long,
and a young man may die soone.
                                        But

Luc. 21.

But if thou be old, not be affraid to
doe penance. Runne as much as thou
canft : for that thou canft not
continue long in this life Know for
certaine, that (according to the ordi-
narie courfe of men) the older thou art,
the fuller thou art of finne. Why therefore doft thou neglect to doe penance
for thy former offences, fithence thou
knoweft that thou art shortly to depart hence? Gods merciee hath long
endured thee, that thou mightft doe
penáce; the fupreme Vmpire hath lóg
expected thine amendement: he hath
giuen thee ample time to fatisfie for
thy finnes. But thou, according to thy
hardnes and impenitent heart, doft
defpife the longanimitie of Gods patience: thou doft not acknowledge
that thou art for borne, that thou
migh ift doe penance : neither doft
thou forfake the finnes of thy youth.
Thou haft pofled ouer the time of thy
youth without doing good workes:
thou continueft in thy wonted vices:
neither doft thou endeauour to begin
to doe penance now at leaft in thine
old age, which thou oughtft to haue

G   done

done long since in thy youth, when
thou hadst greater strength and forces.
Thou farsakest no thy former offences:
thou fearest not auarice, detraction,
and rash censuring of others: and whiles thou fearest not to doe amisse, thou
descendest into hell without doing
penance.

Behold death the cutter off of penance hastneth; behold the end of thy
life approcheth : and thus thou negle-
ctest to make satisfaction for thy sinnes, vntill thou loose both life and
time at once. Tell me, ô thou old and
aged man, why dost thou differre
thine amendment from day to day,
who art not sure to liue vntill to morrow? Thou walkest daily vpon the
brinke of death, and dost thou delay
to be sorowfull for thy sinnes? Thou
sighest now when it is almost to late :
and yet thou dost not forsake that,
which thou sighest at. For thou saiest
(being loaden with old age and vice.)
Woe is me, why haue I spent the flower of my youth so vnfruitfully? Why
haue I delayed to liue vertuously? Why
did I not, when I was young and
strong,

ſtrong, take vpon me the habit of a religious mans? I thought vnhappie man, that old age had beene the fitteſt time to haue done penance: and hoped likewiſe, that which in my you ſeemed hard, would be done with eaſe when I grew old.

But my fooliſhnes hath deceiued me, and I am ſhamefully deceiued. Now I haue learned by experience, that old age is not capable of good manners, but keepeth what it had learned before. Thoſe cuſtomes or habits which a man getteth when he is young and luſtie, remaine ordinarily with him to his dying day. I would faine doe penance now being old, but am not able, for that by reaſon of my former bad cuſtomes; I grone at the verie thought thereof, as at a thing impoſſible. Whatſoeuer I begin contrarie to my wonted cuſtome, I find my ſelfe vnable to performe: becauſe it is a hard thing to meditate new matters in an old mind. Acts of vertue, which in my youth (if I would) ſeemed vnto me eaſie aud facill: appeare vnto me now being old hard and impoſſi-

ble.

ble. Woe be to me, for that that saying
of the wise man is verified in me: A
*young man according to his way; When he
is old, will not depart frhmit.* For old age
is encumbred with many incommo-
dities, from which it is not freed but
by death onely.

Wherefore ô young men, whose age
is apt to endure labours : learne to
inure your selues to vertue and holy
exercices : accustome your selues to
ouercome the desires of the flesh : because he that neglecteth to amend his
life when is young, will, when he is
old, abhorre the same. As euerie
one desireth to be found when he is
old, so let him liue whiles he is
young. For he that addicteth himselfe to vertue in his youth, will
easily perseuere in the same euen
vntill death. Whatsoeuer we learne in
the tender age of our childhood, we
better retaine afterward. But in what
age soeuer a man betaketh himselfe to
penance ; let him know, that in all
things he will haue neede of patience.
For he will feele many temptations
and aduersities, walking in the law of
our

Prou.22

our Lord: of which he was ignorant,
aslong as he went in the way of the
world. A man therefore (of what state
or condition soeuer he be) comming
to Gods seruice, must expect many
temptations and difficulties, against
which he ought to fight in the feare of
our Lord with patience.   For the king- Mat. 11.
dom of God suffereth violence, and the violent beare it away.

He that neglecteth to vse violence
against the temptations of the flesh,
will not depart conquerour, but con-
quered; and is not fit for the kingdome
of God. But what neede is there of so
many words? There is not a iust man
on earth, that is altogether free from
temptations. For the scripture saieth:
Many are the tribulations of the iust : and Psal. 33.
out of all these our Lord will deliuer them.
And an other scripture doth affirme:
That by many tribulations we must enter Act. 14.
into the kingdome of God.

But how patiently all the aduersities
of this present life are to be endured,
the holy Apostle doth tell vs, saying:
The passions of this time are not condigne to Rom. 8.
the glorie to come, that shall be reuealed in
vs.

vs. For whatsoeuer we can endure
heere on earth, is but for a verie short
time: but the reward due to our paſ-
ſions and patience shall be euerlaſting.
If therefore any aduerſitie happen
vnto vs : if any temptation befall vs,
let vs alwayes (being mindfull of our
future recompenſe) embrace patiéce:
knowing that none of theſe things are
of long continuance.

CHAPTER VI.

*Of the manifold miſeries of
man's life.*

SVch, and ſo many are the miſeries
of mans life, that albeit it were e-
ternal and had no end in this world;
yet it is worthily thought worthy by
wiſe men to be contemned. Heerevpon holy Iob ſaieth: *Man borne of a
Woman, liuing a short time, is replenished
With many miſeries. Who as a flower commeth forth and is deſtroyed, and fleeth as a
shade &*

Iob 14.

shadow, and neuer abideth in the same state.
For verily the whole life of man vpon
earth is miserie: to whome life is labour, death danger. How loug therefore ô man, wilt thou loue thine owne
miserie? how long wilt thou loue thy
banishmét in this world? Behold with
how many crosses, troubles and tribulations doth the world persecute thee,
and yet dost thou not consent to be separated from his companie? Man is a
pilgrime or passenger vpó earth, euerie hower part of his way is cut shorter: euerie day he is pushed foreward
to the end of his iourney.

The dayes of man are as the dayes of a Iob 7.
hireling: Euerie moment he draweth
towards the euening: at which time
he shall receiue a recompense for his
paine. He that hath laboured well and
lustilie in our Lord's vineyard, shall
for his labour receiue an euerlasting
reward. Why then do we linger? why
do we stand all the day idle in the market place of this world? Let vs goe into the vine-yard of our Lord: let vs labour as good souldiers of Iesus-Christ:
because if we labour during this short
life

life in fowing the feede of vertue, we
shall doubtlefle reape the fruit of that
celeftial countrie. *But he that foweth*
fparingly, shall alfo reape fparingly. Aflong
as we liue in this life we are wretched,
and fubiect to many tribulations in
the world. For like as paine doth not
make a Mattyr, but the caufe: fo
tribulation doth not merit, but patience.

Both iuft men and wicked haue their
temptations in the world. But aduerfitie to iuft men is turned by patience
into the merit of eternal happines:
contrariwife to wicked men and finners it is reputed as finne by reafon of
their impatience and lewdnes. Tribulation maketh no man blefled; but the
onely loue of God, and patience cau-
feth merit. For finners likewife are
vexed with many miferies in this
world, who notwithftandinge are vt-
terly deuoid of merit. The feare of God
is not before their eies : they fuffer afflictions not for the loue of our Lord,
nor in refpect of heauen, but for that
they know not how to auoid them.
Many are the fcoarges of a finner, but thofe
(onely)

2. Cor. 9

Pfal. 31.

(onely) that hope in our Lord mercie shall compasse.

Sithence therefore no man can liue in this world without tribulation and miserie: let vs make a vertue of necessitie, that so we may turne the euills, which necessarily we endure, to the loue of our Lord and Sauiour. Let vs alwayes acknowledge the miserie of our owne condition, and continuallie be mindfull of the same: to the end, that when we call the same to mind amidst our worldly prosperitie, we may cast aside all pride and vaine securitie. Finally we see by the consideration of our owne basenes, what we ought to thinke of our selues.

We are conceiued and borne in sinne: we are nowrished with labour and paine: we are tossed vp and downe with continual troubles and tribulations. In the interim (ô mortal man) what hope hast thou of redresse? Death onely is the end of miseries But tell me I pray thee, what dost thou expect? The end of miserie. Why then dost thou feare death? For no man before he die, can be happie. Thou desirest

H   that

that the miserie of this life were finish-
hed : and yet the verie thought of
death maketh thee affraid. O miserie,
aud intollerable affliction of spirit. It
is a miserie to liue, and a danger to
die. We abhorre the prison, and yet we
feare to goe forth of the same . What
then shall we doe ? Turne which way
we will, and we find nothing but miserie and trouble.

Behold they that follow the world
are not free from miseries, but are
daily vexed with many tribulations
and anxieties. To what end? With what
fruit ? With what recompence ? That
they may obtaine in the world what
they couet. For the diuel also hath his
martyrs: the world , and carnal pleasures haue likewise theirs. For verily
they that serue the diuel in sinne and
carnal pleasures , endure euen in this
world many miseries : to the end they
may know that from paines temporal,
they are within a while to passe to
those that are eternal. The louers likewise of this world , who hunt after
vaine honours: who seeke after transitorie riches ; who fulfill the desires of
the

the flesh, do daily subiect themselues
to infinite miseries and anxities. Enuie
followeth felicitie: and euerie one sub-
mitteth himselfe to so much the greater danger, by how much the higher
he ascendeth in power. For it must
needes be, that he that is feared by many, doth likewise feare many.

Finally, who is able to expresse the
continual cares and miseries of rich
men? For the wise man saieth: *The sa-* Eccle.5.
tietie of the rich doth not suffer him to
sleepe. Where riches are, there is care.
These are the martyrs of the world:
to whome death is not the end of affliction, but the entrance of eternal tribulation. From smal perplexities they
passe to those that are vnspeakeable:
from paines temporal to paines e ternal: from light tribulations to those
that are most terrible. For to wicked
men and sinners death doth not bring
the end of miserie, but the beginning
of calamitie. Contrariwise, by death
iust men attaine to the period of humane tribulatió. For hauing by dying
finished their life and miserie in this
world: they fortwith begin to liue

happily

happily world without end.

Whosoeuer therefore doth desire to
attaine to the ioyes of eternal happines : who soeuer doth couet to be ad-
mitted into the quires of those heauenly citizens, let him behaue himselfe as
a Martyr of God, and for the loue of
him patiently and humbly endure all
the miseries of this world. For it is better to enter with patience by the miseries of this life into the kingdome of
heauen : then by impatience to be sent
to perpetual damnation. What doth
the short comfort and contentment of
the world profit vs, which is past in a
trice? What do riches, what do honours,
what doth vaine presumption of life
auaile vs ? Woe be to the louers of the
world : woe be vnto rich men, that are
couetous and wicked, who contemning the loue of God, are delighted in
the pleasures of the world.

Why dost thou deceiue thy selfe ô
thou rich glutton? why dost thou daily
kill thine immortal soule by the desires
of the flesh ? Why dost thou put thy
trust in the multitude of thy riches?
Abondance of temporal goods doth
free

free no man from death : carnal pleasures do defend no man from the wormes : neither do worldly honours preserue any man after death from corruption and rottennes. For all earthly
things do perish : and follow no man
after death. That rich man mentioned
in the Gospel, that was clothed with **Luc. 16.**
purple and silke, and fared delitiously
euerie day, being vnmindfull of death
to come, refused to heare the pittifull
crie of the poore man, and therefore
crieth himselfe now in hell, and no
man helpeth him.

Where are now his cellars, which
whilome were replenished with diuersitie of wines? Where are now his
granaries heaped full of corne? Where
is now his table furnished with varie-
rie of daintie dishes? Where is his silke
and purple? All these things haue passed away as a shadow : and the possession of these temporal things hath perished with their possessor. what good
do those riches doe a rish man in hell;
which he hath left behind him in the
world? What do his honours what doth
is faire wife, what do his deare children

dren auaile him ? Purple will defend
no man in hell from cold ; nor silke
from heate, nor gold from wanr There
the affeation of worldly friends shall
ceafe: there carnal alliance and parentage shall perish ; becaufe, euerie one
shall be iudged in his owne wickednes.

Now therefore ô man remember
thy time which is paft and gone, and
know that thou alfo art mortal by
other mens deftruation. Where are thy
progenitors ? Where is thy father and
mother, thy brethren and thy fifters?
Where are thofe ftriplings and boyes,
with whome heeretofore thou haft
played fo many coltish toyes ? Where
are thofe men and woemen, whofe
time thou haft both knowne, and likewife their life and conuerfation?
Where is thy wife, and children? Behold they are dead and gone, and their
remembrance is perished frô amongft
men. What do riches now profit them?
what do honours helpe them? what do
carnal pleafures comfort them.

What do the delights (I fay) of the
world auaile thofe that are dead, for
which

which they are now euerlastingly tormented? Or what harme doth pouertie and tribulatiō suffered in this world
doe to iust men, after that this life is
ended; for which they receiue the ioy
of eternal beatitude? He that is dead
and gone, what good doth it doe him,
to haue liued long? what if thou hadst
liued a thousand yeares vpon earth:
yet thou couldst not escape (although
thou didst deferre) death.

Verily when the hower of death is
come, farewell all worldly pleasure and
pastime. Thou wilt thinke at that
hower, that thy life hath beene most
short: then thou wilt make no account
of thy former recreation and sport;
being then affraid, that thou shalt presently passe to punishment. Then thou
wilt wish that thou hadst forsaken the
world, and wilt say: Wretch that I am,
who haue so lewdly spent my whole
life in sinne : who louing the world,
haue walked after vanities : why did
I not (when I was whole and sound)
feare this hower so full of danger?

O that I had spent my dayes in Gods
seruice; I would to God I had become
a Monke

a Monke in some Monasterie; for then I should die now securely. What do riches now profit me ? What do honours helpe me ? What doth dignitie, nobilitie, or the vaine knowledge of the world auaile me ? I was whilome rich and mightie: I possessed gold and siluer in aboundance ; neither was there any end of my subitance. But what good do all my goods now doe me ? Behold now i die, and am to receiue a sorrowfull sentence, according to the merit of mine actions. My gold in which I trusted, what doth it profit me, sithence it cannot deliuer me from the dominion of death ? Woe be to me wretch. I haue deferred to doe penáce, aslong as I was whole and found : now I lie in my death bed : and albeit I am to depart presently out of this world, yet I cannot fixe my mind vpon any thing that may turne to the good of my soule Now I desire to repent, but am not able.

O cursed cares of the world ! ó vaine and vanishing riches ! ó pestiferous pleasures of the flesh ! I thought my life good enough, if I perseuered in the
Chri-

Christian faith. Howbeit faith is vaine
without good workes anfwerable to
the fame. Now infinite crimes do fal-
lie forth againft me out of the fecret
corners of my confcience: now many
finnes do reprefent themfelues to my
remembrance, of whome a llong as I
was well, I had no fcruple at all. Now
therefore what shall I doe? To whome
shall I flie? O how fecurely should I
now depart out of this world, if I had
walked well and religioufly in the way
of our Lord.

Meditate on thefe things (ô man)
whiles thou art liuing: confider thefe
things whiles thou art healthy and
ftrong: and as thou doft defire to be
found at the hower of thy death, fo
omit not to liue all the dayes of thy
life.

I   CHAP.

CHAPTER VII.

That in euerie state, sexe, age, and condition of this life, miseries and temptations are neuer wanting.

Iob 14.

MAn borne of a woman, liuing a short time, is replenished with many miseries. Who as a flower commeth forth, and is destroyed, and flieth as a shadow, and neuer abideth in the same state. What man? Euerie man. What euerie man? Euerie man is wretched, and his life on earth is short. Why is he wretched? Because he is subiect to corruption, and neuer abideth in the same state. why is his life short? Because he dieth on a sodaine. Is therefore euerie man wretched? Wretched without doubt. Then children are also wretched. Yes, they likewise are wretched. Why wretched? Because men. If therefore all are wretched, who are happie? No man in this life.

life. Of what ftate, fexe, condition, or age foeuer a man is, aflong as he is in this world, he is wretched. Doth death therefore make men bappie ? It doth not make : but difcerne who are happie.

What doth it difcerne ? Betweene the happie and wretched. For all of vs, aflong as we liue in this world, are wretched. But when by death we are deliuered out of this life, we are feuered one from an other, as fifhes that are taken, vpon the shore : for fome of vs being good, are carried to life euerlafting, feeling from thence foreward no miferie at all ; others that are wicked, are fent from temporal miferie to eternal.

For the miferie of this life may be vnderftood after a twofold manner: firft, as it is common to all mē through the neceffitie of nature : fecondly, as it is caufed through fondrie accidents that occurre. By reafon of the neceffi- tie of our corrupt nature we are all wretched : mutable through the inter- change of times and chances : all of vs (aflong as we liue in flesh) are paffible:

I 2   in

in a word all are mortal. Through the
varietie of chances and fortune, miserie
is not equal to all me; but euerie one in
his state, according to the qualitie of
his mind, doth either ouercome, or is
ouercome by temptations. Finally
often times according to our merits
miserie is inflicted vpon vs euen in
this place of pilgrimage : where the
paine is not rewarded, but the cause.
For whosoeuer suffereth for righteous-
nes sake in this world, is not to be
esteemed wretched, but blessed : but
he that sustaineth punishment or per-
secution in this world for his sinnes, is
both miserable and wretched, and altogether estranged from the happines
of the Saincts.

Howbeit it is not the least part of
iustice to endure the miseries of this
life humbly and patiently for the loue
of God. For all things which by nature
seeme necessarie vnto vs, may by the
loue of God be made meritorious. If
therefore for the loue of God we willingly and humbly endure corporal
necessities and miseries ; it is a token
that we draw neere to iustice. To the
end

Wherefore we may become happie
after death in heauen, let vs patiently
obtaine the miseries of this our present
seiourning, turning the instruments of
necessitie into weapons of pietie and
deuotion. For aslong as we liue in this
place of pilgrimage we are necessarily
wretched. The necessitie of suffering is
alike to all mankind, but the end is
much different.

He that for the loue of God can turne
necessitie into a vertue, being by death
let free from earthly miserie, shall merit to obtaine eternal felicitie. But he
that during the time of this life doth
endure the miseries of human condition with impatience : that murmu-
reth against God being enflamed with
the fire brands of his sinnes : doth not
escape miserie after death, but maketh
an exchange. What exchange ? Of his
miserie. Of what miserie ? Temporal.
How doth he change it ? From little
into great, from short into eternal. For
he that perseuering heere in his sinnes,
doth by death end his miserie temporal : being condemned by the iust iudgement of God, entreth into eternal.

And

And he that in th's life doth patiently
for the loue of God suftaine trouble
and tribulation : being freed by death
from all miferie and afflictiõ, raigneth
happily with Chrift after death world
without end, in the land of the Liuing.
For to iuft and good men the dore of
eternal felicitie after death ftandeth
open.

Now therefore for that we muft of
neceffitie endure many miferies and
temptations in this life : let vs ftudie
to turne this neceffitie into a vertue:
that fo we may beare the euills that
betide vs in this world, patiently and
cheerefully for the loue of God.
Neither let any man efteeme himfelfe
free in this life from aduerfitie and miferie : becaufe euerie one is then truly
miferable, when he thinketh himfelfe
happie. No man is free from miferie,
from his verie cradle to his dying day.

In euerie age there is miferie and
trouble, although there are many that
know not that they are miferable.
Whatfoeuer is fubiect to change by
generat.õ and corruption, is truly termed miferable and vaine. Man therefore

fore is miserable : his works are vaine:
he is troubled in vaine. He is conceiued and borne in miserie and sinne:
he is brought vp in continual miserie
and paine : he liueth and dieth after
the same fashion. To conclude, euerie
age, state, and condition is troubled
and tormented with miserie and temptation.

Who is able perfectly to vnfold the
miseries of infancie and child hood ? A
man is miserable assoone as he is conceiued in his mothers wombe : and in
danger of death, before he euer see the
light of heauen. He is conceiued in original sinne, ād borne the child of wrath
by reason of the corrupt roote , from
whence he hath his beginning. Finally
before he begin to draw vital breath ,
he approcheth towards death. But of
these things we shall speake in some
other place.

No man liuing in this vale of miserie , is altogether free from aduersitie.
Both infancie, youth, and old age, haue
each of them their miseries. Likewise
in each state, there is miserie and affliction of spirit. The Pope albeit the
supreme.

supreme Bishop and Chrifts Vicar on
earth, is fubiect in this life to many
troubles and vexations: and by how
much the more he is exalted aboue all
others in dignitie, by fo much the more
he is replenifhed with miferie. For
from the greateft Prince to the pooreft
peafant, there is no man vpon earth
without miferie and vexatiō of mind.
For the whole world (which way
foeuer thou doft caft thine eies) is full
of bitternes and anguifh. If thou
enter into religion, thou fhalt find affliction: if thou remaine in the world,
thou wilt find the fame. If thou become
learned in all manner of fciences, thou
wilt find miferie in all thefe, for that
(according to the affertion of the Prea-
Eccl. 1. cher.) *He that addeth knowledge, addeth
also labour.* Although thou be neuer fo
great, rich, and potent: yet thou wilt
not want vexation of mind. Neither
are thofe void of miferie, that are moft
poore and abiect, who for the moft
part are by fo much the more vnfortunate, for that they doe not know
themfelues to be wretched. Hufband-
men likewife that employ themfelues
in

in neceſſarie toyling and tillage, are
ſubiect to many miſeries. Euerie ſtate
therefore of this preſent life is full of
many temptations and miſeries.

O vanitie of vanities: why doſt thou
thinke thy ſelfe happie ? Euerie one
doth miſlike his owne ſtate and condi-
tió, and deſireth that of an other man.
Few are content with their owne
boundes. He that hath bound himſelfe
faſt in the bondes of matrimonie,
ſigheth for ſorow : and would faine
(if he knew how) get himſelfe free,
and commendeth the ſingle life of ſuch
as liue in a Monaſterie. He abhorreth
what he hath, and coueteth what; he
hath not. An other that hath bound
himſelfe to a Monaſtical profeſſion,
hateth his order, habit, and religion, he
reuoketh his intention, diſliketh that
holy courſe of life, that he liueth in;
and extolleth the felicitie of married
men. But why do I vſe ſo many wordes
in a matter ſo well knowne ? Euerie
one imagineth an other mans fortune, better then his owne. And this
alſo is vanitie, and affliction of ſpirit.

All humane states (beleeue me)
from the first to the last, haue their miseries: and oftimes where men hope
to find most happines. there they find
most heauines. Those that are Prelates
and superiours ouer others, commend
the secure and quiet estate of their in-
feriours: contrariwise, those that are
constrayned to liue in subiection,
thinke themselues wretched, and the
others happie men. But we are all deceiued exceedingly: who imagin that
there is any estate of life in this world
void of miserie. Euerie where in the
world there is temptation and miserie:
neither can any man before death be
truly termed happie.

CHAPTER VIII.

*Of the breuitie of this present life, and
the necessitie of death.*

Iob 14.   Man liuing but a short time, is vexed
in this life with many and almost
con-

continual miseries: to the end, that by
the temptations, which he endureth
in this world, he may hasten to come
to the ioyes of eternal beatitude. For
the scripture saieth. *That by many tribu-* Act. 14.
lations we must enter into the kingdome of
God. The time of our life vpon earth is
most short, and subiect to sondrie calamities. He that to day liueth whole
and found ; will perchance be dead to
morrow, and layed vnder ground.
Why then dost thou grow proud, ô
earth and ashes ? Why dost thou not
acknowledge thy selfe to be mortal?
Or if thou dost alreadie know it, why
art thou not fearefull ? Thou canst not
remaine long in this life, for that thou
dost daily hasten towards death. Why
art thou puffed vp with vaine honours,
sithence thou art shortly to be meate
for wormes ? Why dost thou esteeme
thy selfe rich, sithence thou knowest
full weil, that within a while thou
must become poore and miserable.
Why dost thou vaunt of worldly arts
and sciences, sithence thou art shortly
to loose all thy senses ? Why dost thou
bragge of thy beautie and feature,
K 2   seeing

seeing that after a while thou wilt be a most vile carcasse, lying stinking in thy sepulcher?

O blind foolishnes of humane condition! Why dost thou not acknowledge thy selfe miserable, ô mortal man? Thou thinkest thy selfe rich and fortunate, and dost not reflect how neere death is at hand. Death standeth at thy dore, and maketh haste to hasten thee to thy sepulcher. Why dost thou presume of thy earthly power and might, sithence *all power is of short life.* Art thou a Bishop? Thou wilt quickly die, and an other will be exalted to thy place and dignitie. Where are thy predecessors? Where is he that was next before thee? They are all dead and gone, ãd thou art risen in their roome. Thou canst not long continue, but must shortly follow them that are gone before.

Art thou Abbot or Prior of a Monasterie? Thou wilt not long so continue. Death will come, and is alreadie comming a pace: who will giue thy Priorship to an other, and present thee to the supreme iudge, to be examined of thy

Eccli.
10.

thy carriage and behauiour. What will thy short authoritie then profit thee, which is loſt ſo ſodainely ? What will thine Epiſcopal dignitie, or paſtorall reuerence then auaile thee ? For verily thou ſhalt then be preſented before Chriſt the ſupreme paſtor and iudge, and ſhalt render an accompt to him of all his ſheepe cōmitted to thy charge. At that day thou wilt know, that it will be imputed to the fault of the ſhepheard; if God the ſupreme paſtor find leſſe profit in his flock then he expected. For *euerie one, to whome much was giuen, much ſhall be required of him.* As many men as thou haſt now vnder thy care and gouerment : for ſo many ſheepe ſhalt thou giue an accompt at the day of iudgement. For thou art not onely to render a reckoning to God for thine owne ſoule in particular, but for the ſoules of as many, as in this life haue beene committed to thy care.

Reg. S. Ben. cap. 2.

Luc. 12.

O that thou wouldſt now place that day before the eies of thy mind; ô that thou wouldſt now foreſee thoſe things that are like to befall thee in the end: for then without doubt thou wouldſt

easily

eafily contemne the vaine honours of
the world. Behold death doth haften:
behold thine end is at hand: and thy
regiment and authoritie draweth towards ã end. If therefore thou be wife;
if thou feare the danger of thy foule,
remember thy former offences, and
let the dreadfulnes of death neuer depart from thy remembrance. For the
Eccli.7. wife man faieth: *In all thy Workes remember thy later ends, and thou wilt not
finne for euer.* Nothing doth fo recall a
man from the vanities of the world,
nothing doth fo mortifie the defires of
the flesh, as the often and earneft me-
S. Hier. ditation of death. He eafily (faieth S.
ad Pau- Hierome) contemneth the world, who
linum. alwaies thinketh that he is shortly to
die. Hence Salomon moued through
the confideration of the certainty of
Eccl.2. death, faieth: *Laughter I haue reputed errour, and to ioy I haue faid:* *Why art thou*
Eccle.7. *deceiued in vaine.* Wherefore *it it better to*
goe to the house of mourning, thẽ to the house
of banquetting. For in the one a mã is put
in mind of his ẽd: but in the other there
is no thought of any such thing.

What if a men liue many yeares vpon
earth?

earth ? What if he be rich, mightie, or of noble birth; Death feareth not the auctoritie of earthly power: respecteth not riches: neither is daunted with the nobilitie of gentrie and honour. His proceeding is alike towards all men: he taketh away all without acception of persons : and spareth not so much as one. We must all die; we must all be drawne to Chrifts tribunal, there to be examined, and rewarded according to our merits, good or euill: to remaine long in this life is a thing impoffible.

Let no man therefore deceiue himselfe : let no man presume of worldly honours: let no man truft in the multitude of his riches. Let euerie one prepare himselfe to die well by a vertuous life and conuerfation : let no man hope to liue long, feeing it is a thing vncertaine : becaufe by how much the longer euerie one liueth in this world, by fo much the more vnwilling he is to die, when he groweth old. Why foe? Becaufe the more our liues are prolonged, the more (for the moft part) our finnes are encreafed. For oftentimes
he

he that is feene readie and willing to
die in his young age: is found vnprouided and vnwilling to die euen in his
dotage. Together with our life encrea-
feth the defire thereof: and the more a
man doth haften towords death , the
more he loueth life. For a young man
feareth death the leffe , for that he
knoweth that he hath offended but in
a few things. But when mans life is ex-
tended to old age ; it is ordinarily defiled vith many vices and finnes: and
feareth death by fo much the more,by
how much the more it knoweth to
haue offended in many things.

Man of his owne nature is fraile and
prone fo vice ; in fo much , that ordinarily he paffeth ouer that time in plea
fure, and fenfualitie , which he ought
to employ in workes of vertue. Man
longeth to haue his life prolonged:and
whiles he lingereth to doe penance
for his former offences , he feareth to
die vnprouided. He defireth (miferable
wretch) to liue awhile in this world;
and yet men fee, that the longer he is
permitted to remaine in this life , the
leffe he amendeth his manners. He de-
                              fireth

fireth to be old, but refuseth to be so called. He would faine by many yeares attaine to old age; aud when he hath liued so long, that his head is growne white and hoarie; yet still he feareth to issue forth of the bodie.

O how miserable is mans state and condition! Why art thou deceiued in vaine, ô mortal man? How long dost thou not acknowledge that thou art to die? Thou liuest amisse, and therefore no maruail, if death be dreadfull vnto thee. Thou hast refused to wipe away the sinnes of thy youth by penance: thou hast not beene affraid frō time to time to encrease thine offéces, and therefore art vnwilling to appeare before the internal iudge. But thou fearest in vaine, thy feare little profiteth: for that thou canst not escape death. Thou demandest a longer space to doe penance: and albeit the terme of thy life be neuer so long prorogued, yet thou dost not amend. What good doth long life doe thee, which weareth away wholy, in sinne and miserie? What do many yeares, void of good workes, auaile thee?

L   O how

O how seldome do old men grow better: they alwayes adde new vices to their former: they alwayes grow worse and worse in their conuersation, and tend towards death vnsetled in their resolutiō. For those things which our mind is inured vnto in our youth, we hardly leaue aslong as we liue vpon earth. For it is verie hard to forsake those things to which we are accusto-med, and to meditate new things in an old mind.

What a young man hath learned, he will be loath to leaue, when he is old. He that is negligent by deferring his good purposes of amendment, loofeth euē hese likewife in the end. Behold we deferre to doe penance whiles we are whole & found: we procrastinate frō day to day the time of our amendment: and whiles we couet to liue longer in the world, being ouertaken by death vnawares, we depart out of this life without repentáce. We daily meditate of the amendment of our liues: to morrow we thinke to begin: but aslōg as we neglect to vse, violence to our bad customes, we alwaies perseuere in
sinne.

finne. For no man can rife from his bad cuftomes, that doth not vfe violence to himfelfe againft the defires of the flesh. He erevpon it is written of Pharao in Exodus : *The heart of Pharao is hardned : he Will not difmiffe the people, but in a ftrong hand, and ftretched out arme.* Who is vnderftood by Pharao, but the diuell, who keepeth obtinate finners in bondage, as flaues to his will? For he is the head of all the wicked : in fo much, that whome he hath once fubie-cted to his empire of bad cuftome, he permitteth not to flie to the remedies of penance, but in a ftrong hand, and ftretched out arme. What meane you by a ftrong hād, or ftretched out arme? Liften, and I will tell you. A ftrong hand doth fignifie the grace of God almigh-tie : without whofe affiftance no mā can rife to doe penance. For verily he that is once fallen into the pit of finne, without Gods efpecial fauour cannot rife againe.

No man is able to ftand before his fall into finne, except almightie Gods grace preuent him by preferuing him: no man is able to rife after he is fallen,

L 2   vnleffe

Exod. 7.

vnleſſe almightie Gods mercie erect
him by aſſiſting him. But what good
doth free will doe then? What good
doth a ſtretched out arme? Liſten. Free
will is neceſſarie for the accompli-
shing of euerie good worke: by which
the grace of God doth worke in vs
Philip.2 *Both to Will and to accomplish*, according
to his good will. Like as a worke-man
worketh and perfecteth his worke by
a fit inſtrument : ſo the grace of God
diſpoſeth and affecteth good workes
in mé by free will. & like as free will
profiteth nothing without the grace
of God: ſo the grace of God requireth
our free will to doe that which is good.

Heerevpon the holy Apoſtle writing
2. Cor.6 to the Corinthians, ſaieth : *We exhort*
you, that you receiue not the grace of God
in vaine. Is then the grace of God receiued now and then in vaine? Yes verily in vaine. When doth this happen?
hearkē. Whoſoeuer doth neglect to doe
penance whiles he is healthy and ſtróg
whoſoeuer doth cótemne to doe good
whiles he can, receiueth the grace of
God in vaine. For this cauſe it is ſaid:
Exod.7. *He Will not diſmiſſe my people, but in a ſtróg*
hand

hand, *and stretched out arme*: that is, in Gods grace, & mans free will. Stretch forth thine arme: Gods grace is in readinesse. Stretch him forth (Isay) leaft thou loose both grace, and time to doe penance. Why doft thou delay? Why doft thou linger? Why doft thou wauer? Why art thou troubled with vaine cogitations? *The kingdome of heauen suffereth violence.* Mat.11.

How long doft thou delay thy conuerfion? How long doft thou receiue the grace of God in vaine? Why doft thou not demand a ftrong hand for thy deliuerie? Why doft thou not voluntarily stretch forth the arme of thy will to the grace of God almightie, voluntarily offering it felfe to affift thee? Why doft thou not come when God calleth thee? Why doft thou linger? No vertue is gotté without labour: neither are euill cuftomes fubdued without great trauail and fweat. Heauen is obtained, not by the defires of the flesh, but of the fpirit.

Howbeit no man is able to conquer the defires of the flesh, but he that (aided by Gods grace) knoweth how
to

to vse violence, to himselfe, What vio-
léce? Listen to our Lords owne wordes.
Mat. 16. He that Will, faith he, come after me, let him
take vp his crosse, and follow me. In this our
violence doth consist: in this is contained the chiefe point of the conquest.
If thou desire by victorie ouer thy flesh
to attaine to eternal beatitude, contemne thine owne will for the loue of
God. Walke according to the spirit:
and by this meanes thou wilt easily
subdue the desires of the flesh. Neuerthelesse notwithstanding all this, omit
not daily to take vp thine owne crosse,
if thou desire to follow our Lord to
perpetual happines. What crosse do
you meane? The crosse of daily temptation. And how then is it to be borne?
By patience in tribulation. For our
Luc. 21. Lord saieth to his followers. In your patience you shal possesse your soules. And
the holy Apostle saieth, writing to the
Heb. 10 hebrewes: Patience is necessarie for you:
that doing the Will of God, you may receiue
the promise.

Now therefore stretch forth the
arme of thy free will, if thou desire to
escape the darke Ægypt of hell. Why
dost

dost thou feare? Why dost thou linger?
Why dost thou stagger? Why dost thou
wauer? Why dost thou not begin to day
to doe penance, and liue vertuously:
sithence thou art not ignorant, that
thou must shortly die? Behold death
the cutter off of penance commeth on
a pace; who will finish thy life and thy
good purposes of liuing well both at
once.

CHAPTER IX.

Of the bitternes of death, and the strict
accompt that must be giuen in our
last iudgement.

OF all terrible things, death is the
most terrible : which snatcheth
the soule out of the bodie with surpassing great paine and anguish : which
bringeth the flesh into dust and ashes:
and sendeth the spirit to the tribunal
seate of Christ, there to be iudged according to his deserts. True it is, that
death

Aristot.
3.Ethics

death is determined for all : yet to sinners onely, it is terrible and fearefull. For a iust man, if he be preuented with death, shalt be in a place of refreshing. But with the wicked it goeth cleane contrarie : to whome death addeth an end of their temporal prosperitie, and a beginning of their eternal calamitie. Woe be to hard-hearted sinners : who whiles they neglect to doe penance, descend into hell there to remaine in euerlasting torments.

What do earthly riches auaile those that are thus tormented in hell ? What content haue thy now of their former worldly honours, or most filthy pleasures of the flesh ? What good doth the glorie of the world now doe them, or the maiestie of a kingdome ; All these thing are past away ; and vanished out of sight, like the smoke of a chimney. Wicked men lie burning in hell fire, there to be tormented for euer. Where are the carnall pleasures which they loued so deare ? Where is their hope of liuing longer ? Where is their good purpose of doing penance, put off for so many yeares together ? Their plea-

sure

sure is cháged into eternal paine: their
hope into confusion, their good purposes into blasphemie and reuiling.
Now from the dead as nothing confession is   Eccl.17.
perished: The purpose of repentance is
vanished: the time of doing good is
expired.

Blessed is the man, that is alwayes feare-   Prou.28
full: Who considereth the bitternes of
death by daily thinking thereof now
before hand: who by penance prepareth himselfe against the comming of
the eternal iudge. For nothing doth so
stirre vp the mind to compunction:
nothing doth so mortifie the desires of
the flesh: nothing doth so moue a man
to doe penance; as the frequent and
earnest meditation of death. So Eze-   4. King.
chias king of Iewrie, being told that   20.
he was to die, turning to the wall,
wept and lamented: and by his teares
got to haue his life prolonged. So the   Ion.3.
Niniuites hearing our Lord threaten
the subuersion of their citie, feared exceedingly: and being sorrowfull for
their sinnes, made haste to doe penance
in sack-cloth and ashes, and by
this meanes saued both their citie and
M   them-

3.King.
21.

themselues. So Achas king of Israel hearing the sentence of death, hanging downe his head towards the earth, humbled himselfe, who before had proudly despised the speeches of Elias. There is no man so proud and cruel, who by seriously thinking of death, doth not become meeke and gentle.

Wherefore be alwayes mindfull of thy end: forget not thy last iudgement, if thou desire to ouercome the vaine enticements of the world. For he that seriously considereth ; that he shall shortly die, loueth nothing in the world that is transitorie. Certainely the attentiue memorie of death causeth a mã to despise the world: to loath carnal pleasures, and to conténe earthly riches. For the mind is easilie induced to the contempt of all transitorie content, if it carefully meditate of death as present. Finally if we diligently consider the dangers, that then are like to befall vs, doubtlesse we shall scarce abstaine from teares.

The diuell is most busie at the hower of our death to entrap vs: for that he
knov-

knoweth that from thence foreward
he shall haue no more occaſiō to ouercome vs. For that enemie of mankind
knoweth that our reward doth depend
on the end of enr labour : & therefore
at the hower of our death aſſaulteth
vs with ſo much the greater violence,
leaſt a man remaine conſtant in his
good purpoſes. And therefore we read
that many holy men haue at the hower
of their death beene verie much affraid :for that they were not ignorant,
that the ſumne of their ſaluation did
depend on that laſt period. What ſhall
we poore wretches doe at that hower,
that are ſo ſinfull and fraile; ſithence
Sainčts and perfečt men do quake and
tremble ? What maruaile is it , if the
rafters be rent and riuen , when the
great pillars of the houſe are ſoe cruelly ſhaken ? If Sainčts and iuſt men
feare , what ſhall ſinners and wicked
men doe at that hower ?

Wo be to vs. We miſpend the time
allotted to doe penance? and yet haſten towards death, as if we were ſecure of our future recompenee. Howbeit he is deceiued , that expečteth

death

death without amendment. He that liueth amisse, doth neuer die well without repentance. It is said, that when
our Sauiour hanged on the crosse for
the redemption of mankind, the enemie of mans saluation was there present; to the end, that he that could find
no sinne in our Lord during his life,
might find some thing at the hower of
his death. Who now is not affraid, if
he consider the craft of the subtill enemie of mankind? The diuel heeretofore appeared to S. Martin at the
hower of his death, seeking some thing
whereof to accuse him. To whome the
blessed man replied : Why dost thou
stand heere thou cruel beast? Whome
dost thou expect? Depart : thou shalt
find no filth in me. To which wordes
the diuel is reported to haue replied
with indignation and furie : When the
sonne of God died on the crosse, I was
present, and must I not approach neere
to thee? There was neuer yet any man
died, to whome at the hower of death
I was not present. Heerevpon holy
men albeit they do continually feare
Gods iudgements in all their actions,

Sulpi-
tius in
his life.

yet

yet then they feare moſt of all, when
they ſee, that hauing paied nature her
due, they muſt ſhortly be preſented
before Chriſts tribunal. And their feare
is ſo much the greater, by how much
their eternal retribution draweth
neerer.

What ſhall we poore wretched wormes doe when we come to die, who
are void of all ſanctitie ? Let vs therefore feare death moſt aſſuredly comming, that we may not feare the ſame
when it is come. For nothing is more
certaine then death : nothing in this
world more cruel, nothing more terrible. And albeit we are all moſt aſſured
of death approaching : yet we know
not at what hower it will come, nor in
what ſtate it will find vs at its comming. Wherevpon our Lord doth ad-
moniſh vs in the Goſpel, ſaying.
Watch ye therefore: for you know not the   **Mat.25.**
day, nor the hower. And bringing a ſimi-
litude vpon this, he ſayeth : *Let your*   **Luc.12.**
loines be girded, and candles burning in your
handes, and you like to men expecting their
Lord, when he ſhall returne from the mar-
riage: that when he doth come and knock,

forth-

forth with they may open vnto him. Blessed are those seruants, Who when our Lord commeth, he shall find Watching.

Who is this Lord ? Christ Iesus the eternal iudge. Who is the seruant ? Euerie Christian man. When commeth this Lord ? When a Christian by death is to depart out of this world When knocketh he ? When by sicknes he biddeth any one prepare himselfe to die. Who is he that watcheth at our Lords comming . He that in the loue and feare of God keepeth the house of his conscience cleane from sinne. Which is the dore of this house ? It is the conscience. When doth the seruant open to his Lord knocking ? When by good workes he is readie for death approaching What reward shall that seruant haue that watcheth, and openeth to his Lord comming ? Ouer all things which he possesseth, he shall appoint him. To what end ? That he may happily reioyce with all the holy Angells and Saincts world without end. Who promiseth thus much ? The Sauiour of the world, that willeth vs to watch. Where doth he intimate vnto vs this

his

his will? In his holy Gofpel. Who
watcheth laudably? He, that ferioufly
confidering that he muft die, cleanfeth
his foule from all finne and iniquitie.
Which is the beft method or meanes to
cleanfe our felues? Charitie, and practice of penance. For we offend all in   Iac.3.
many things. And vnleffe we daily cor-
rect our felues by penance, we shall
find our felues at the hower of death
but in a bad cafe.

Woe be to me, for that I haue not
watched, as it behoued a good feruat.
What shall I now doe frō hence foreward? Liften to our Lord calling thee
and expecting vntill an other watch.
Haft thou neglected the firft watch?
Be more carefull at the fecond. What
is the firft watch? Our child-hoode.
What if the feruant neglect this firft?
Let him haue a care to be readie at the
fecond. What is the fecond watch?
Youth or young age. What if the feruant neglect this likewife? Let him obferue the third with all care and dili-
géce. What is the third? Old age. What
if he alfo neglect this? Then doubtleffe
he shalbe reckoned amongft the foolish

lish virgins. Which foolish virgins?
Those; who being addicted to drousi-
nes and lasines went to meete the celestial bridegroome without oile in their
lampes. For sinners, who sleepe and
take their ease in carnal pleasures, cō-
temne to make themselues readie by
holy exercises to goe meete our Lord,
and therefore are compelled by death
to descend into hell with their lampes
extinguished. To whome crauing entrance into the kingdome of heauen,
Mat.25. this answere was made by our Lord:
Amen I say vnto you, I know you not.

Let vs therefore watch (deare brethren) whiles we haue time:let vs prepare our selues to meete our Lord before he come : least, with the foolish
virgins, we be excluded out of the
Luc. 12. kingdome of heaue.*Let our loines be girded, and candles burning in our handes*; to
the end we may restraine our flesh frō
pleasures and delightes ; and inwardly
before God,and outwardly before mē,
may shine with the light of good workes. Let vs diligently call to mind the
example of the faithfull seruant ,that
was found watching : and let vs daily
                              obserue

obſerue our watch with all are and cir-
cumſpection.

A carefull ſeruant of our Lord ſtan-
ding vpon his cuſtodie doth carefully
thinke of his comming: and by the
candle of well-doing preparerh himſelfe to meete him, and expecteth euerie hower at the dore vntill he come.
He caſteth aſide all other ſollicitude a
farre off from him : he attendeth to his
owne watch and cuſtodie alone : and
couragiouſly like a man, contemneth
the vaine boyiſh toyes that are played
about him. But if in the interim whyle
he expecteth , being ouercome
through heauines , he chance to fall a
ſleepe , leaning his head as it were
againſt the wall: he immediatly rou-
ſeth himſelfe vp to his watch, shaking
off ſleepe by thinking of his Lords ar-
riual: and feareth leaſt his Lord should
knock neuer ſo little. And when at
length after long delay he ſeeth his
Lord comming a farre off: he is ſurpri-
zed with no ſmall feare, leaſt entring
into his houſe, he find any thing that
may moue him to diſpleaſure: neuer-
theleſſe he looſeth not the confidence

N   of

of a good keeper. He goeth therefore
with alacritie to meete his Lord comming : yea he feareth his comming,
albeit he doth not know any thing,
that is Lord can obiect againſt him.

Eccle.9.   Wherevpon the wiſe man ſaieth: *Man
kno Weth not Wheher he be Worthy of loue
or hatred : but all things for reſerued of the
time to come.* Howbeit a faithfull ſeruāt
being readie to meete his Lord knocking by death at the dore of his bodie
although he know himſelfe vnprofitable and to haue done nothing that is
prayſe worthy, yet he diſtruſteth not of
his Lords clemencie: but being placed
betweene hope and feare, he committeth himſelfe confidently to his mer-
Prou.14   cie. For the holȳ Scripture ſaieth. *A
iuſt man hopeth in his death.*

  And although euerie man ought
more to feare. then to hope during
his life : yet when he commeth to die,
let him aſſume a greater confidence of
Gods mercie : leaſt perchance being
deceiued by the diuell through ouer
much feare, he caſt himſelfe head-long
into the pit of deſpaire. For the ſworne
enemie of manking vſeth many
                          deuices

deuices to deceiue mé at their laft end:
and then he sheweth his greateft furie,
when the laft combat is fought for an
eternal victorie.

But in vaine do we feare death, which
we cannot auoid. Heerevpon the wife
man doth admonish vs, faying. *Feare* Eccl.41.
not the iudgement of death. As if he should
plainely fay: Do not feare that, which
thou canft not efcape: neither augmét
thy danger by fearing, leaft thou grow
to defpaire of thy faluation. But what?
Is not death then to be feared? Yes of
fuch as are wicked and reprobate: to
whome it openeth the entrace to hell.
But of fuch as are good and vertuous,
it is to be feared as a motiue to reftraie
them from finne, not to ouerthrow
their conftancie and good refolution.

Howbeit a difcreete meditation of
death is good and profitable for all
forts of people: whofe remembrance
doth preferue the good and righteous
in their good purpofes: and recall finners vnto penance. For to iuft and holy men death is an entrance vnto life
euerlafting: according as the Apoftle
auoucheth, faying: *Vnto me to liue is* Philip.1
Chrift

Christ : and to die is gaine. Why gaine?
Becaufe by death I paffe from forrow
to gladnes ; from trauaile to quietnes:
from contempt to glorie : from pouertie to vnfpeakeable plentie:from feare
to fecuritie: from the world to heauen:
from death to life euerlafting.

But this confidence doth onely be-
feeme fuch as are perfect : to whome
this world is crucified, and they to the
world. Vnhappie Trithemius that I am:
who shall deliuer me from the bodie
of his death? This prefent life is irk-
fome to me, and yet I am affraid to die.
I defire to be diffolued, and to be with
Christ:howbeit I am affraid to appeare
before that internal iudge, whome I
know that I haue offeded by my manifold finnes. The time of my feiourning
feemeth teadious vnto me, for that I
fee, that I do not goe foreward in the
way of vertue ; and therefore I figh
and grone with the Apoftle, faying:
Rom. 7. I know that there dwelleth not in me, that is
to fay, in my flesh, good. For to Will is prefent
With me : but to accomplish that Which is
good, I find not. For not the good Which I
Will, that doe I : but the euill Which I Will
not,

not, that I doe. If the holy Apostle could say this of himselfe, what shall we poore wretches doe? Woe be to vs: who now and then, haue neither power to will nor to accomplish.

O if the strict examination of the internal iudge were neuer absent from the eies of our mind: ô if the remembrance of our later ends did neuer depart from our cogitatiōs: then doubtlesse the world would seeme vile vnto vs, and the bitternes of penance would please vs. How seuere almightie God is in iudging mens sinnes, doth appeare by many examples. For there is no sinne so little, for which there is not assigned a grieuous punishment, if it be not in this life purged by penance. Let vs diligently call to mind what is written of the two Sainct̄s of God Seuerinus Archbishop of Colen, and Paschasius Deacon of the Church of Rome; who being both glorious by miracles testifying their sanctitie, were notwithstanding after death seene in the paines of Purgatorie: the first, for that being busied in the affaires of the common wealth, he had now and then
negli-

negligently performed the canonical howers: the other, for that in the election of Pope Symmachus, he consented not (albeit out of a good zeale) to the desire and opinion of others.

What shall we doe poore wretches, if Saincts goe to Purgatorie, that haue beene famous for doing of miracles? What shall we doe, I say, that are full of iniquitie : if Saincts after death are tormented in Purgatorie ? How shall wicked men escape paine, if Saincts haue not beene ableto escape the same? Let vs therefore feare, deare brethren, and by fearing be carefull in our comportment ; least by negligence we incurre the like punishment. Let vs continually doe penance, for that in this life onely penance can profit vs : when we may not onely escape Purgatorie, but also merit a crowne of glorie.

CHAP.

CHAPTER X.

That through the consideration of death and iudgement : the world, the flesh, and all the pleasures of this præsent life are to be contemned.

THe holy Scripture doth admonish *Eccli. 7* vs saying: *Remēber the last things.* And Moyses speaking of the froward and peruerse natiō of the Iewes, vseth these words: *A nation without counsel it is, and Deut. 32 without wisdome : O that they were wise, and vnderstood, and would prouide for their later ends.* What later ends? Those which follow this presēt life. What are those? Death, and iudgement. Now how profitable the remembrance of death is to a man, the wise man doth declare, saying: *In all thy workes remember thy later Eccli ends, and thou wilt not sinne for euer.*

Behold death doth hasten : the seuere iudgement of God is at hand. How long therefore, ô wretch, dost thou

pre

pretend excuses? How long dost thou
mispend thy time in slouth and negligence? How long wilt thou deferre to
doe penance? thou canst not liue long
in this world: thou wilt shortly be
drawne to the iudgemét seate of God,
where thou art like to receiue a heauie
sentence for thy sinnes ãd negligences
committed.

Now therefore whiles thou art liuing, and in health, doe penance : a-
mend thy manners : cleanse thy conscience. Whatsoeuer thy hand is able to doe,
Worke instantly : for neither Worke, nor
reason, nor Wisdome, nor knowledge shall
be in hell, Whether thou dost hasten. Now is
the time to labour, now are the dayes
to doe penance : in which we may
make satisfaction for our sinnes, by
holy exercises; and by smal works obtaine eternal happines. The world passeth, and the concupiscence thereof:
men die, and turne to corruption, and
are quite forgotten, as if they had neuer beene. Why dost thou trust in thy
gold, ô thou that art wealthy? Why
dost thou vaunt of thy power and authoritie? Why dost thou not consider,

that

that thou muſt ſhortly die ? Let downe
the top ſaile of thy ſtatelines, caſt aſide
all vaine confidence.

Death feareth not honours, reſpe-
cteth not riches, nor reuerenceth gray
haires. Death behaueth himſelfe alike
towards all men : he ſpareth no man,
he honoureth no man. As the ſeruant,
ſo is the maiſter with him : he careth
no more for a king then for a clowne;
and layeth aſwell princely ſcepters, as
plough ſhares leuel with the ground.
He pronounceth iuſt ſentence, and
maketh no acception of perſons. he
demandeth no mans good will : but
denounceth a neceſſitie to all. He doth
not reflect, whether a man be readie to
die, or not. Him for whome he commeth, he carrieth away ſpeedily, neither will he tarrie, although you proffer
him neuer ſo great a ſomme of money.
All the dayes that a man liueth vpon
earth, he haſtneth towards death : and,
as one blind folded goeth a pace towards his end. No age is ſafe from
death : no time ſecure : no place vnder
heauen is exempt from this danger.
Age doth not excuſe a mã that is dying:

O   time

time doth not free him : no place,
though neuer so strong, preserue him.

Sithence therefore in euerie age,
time, and place we are subiect to death,
let vs continually expect the same prepared that watcheth and obserueth vs
euerie moment. The doubtfull, vncertaine, and variable state or condition
of mankind vpon earth , doth suffi-
ciently admonish vs, to haue a care to
prouide for death , and neuer to presume vainely of our selues. For the
Prou.28 scripture saieth : *Blessed is the man, that*
is alwayes fearefull : but he that is of an ob-
stinate mind, shall fall into euill. For certai-
ly he that feareth deathes comming,
keepeth himselfe from all negligence,
asmuch as humane frailtie will permit
him : and striueth, asmuch as he can,
to be found readie for the same.

Who then is rightly affraid to die?
He that by fearing liueth vertuously.
The remembrance of death maketh
wicked men to tremble and feare : but
yet (notwithstanding their feare) they
liue as lewdly as they did before. Feare
doeth no good, where there is no amed-
ment. For the rich men of this world
feare

feare death verie much, becaufe they are loath to depart from their earthly defires, for that they loue nothing but worldly riches. He that hath a guiltie confcience, feareth the comming of the iudge. For he that doth amiſſe, hateth the light : and feareth to be rebuked and corrected for his fault. But what doth it auaile vs to be vnwilling? Neceſſitie vrgeth vs foreward towards our end, neither is the will of man able to withſtand the fame. After death followeth iudgement : wherein our confcience shall accuſe vs as witnes; and iuſtice it felfe shall adiudge vs.

Wherefore whiles we liue in flesh, let vs prudently feare death: let vs prepare our felues by being fearefull, becaufe to efcape it, is a thing impoſſible. Let vs doe penance for our finnes paft, and heereafter carrie our felues more carefully: and endeauour fo to liue, as that we may not feare to die. A good confcience is alwayes full of gladnes, for that it hopeth in Gods aſſiſtance, by humbly obferuing his cōmaundements. But *faluation is farre from finners:* Pfa. 118 who hūt after worldly honoures: who

O 2   delight

delight in auarice, and seeke continually after carnal pleasures. Such as
those feare death, and not without iust
cause: for that they want the testimonie of a good conscience. For like as
death to the good is the entrance from
pouertie to a kingdome: so to wicked
worldly men it is the passage frō pleasure to perdition.

In the meane while, blessed is the
man, that is alwayes fearefull: that
loueth not worldly vanities: that contemneth transitorie riches: that ffleth
the desires of the flesh: that with a
meek prompt obedience obserueth
Gods commaundements. He that is
such a one, expecteth death securely:
hauing a confidence in Gods onely
grace and mercie. For no man becommeth a Sainct by his owne forces: but
it is God that worketh all in all; who
of his infinite goodnes and compassion
vouchsake to grant vs life euerlasting.
Amen.

FINIS.

A
GODLY SHORT
TREATISE, INTITVLED,
THE GOLDEN
MIRROVR
OF
A SINNE-FVLL
SOVLE.

The contents of the chapters of this booke.

A godly short Treatise, intituled,
The golden Mirrour of a
sinnefull soule.

THE PREFACE.

Vanitie of vanities, said Ecclesiastes, and all things vanitie. Sithence according to the assertion of that egregius doctor S. Gregorie, There is not a more acceptable sacrifice to God, then the zeale of soules, (that is a desire of doing them good) for this reason I haue collected this short Treatise following, out of the workes of diuerse holy Doctors of the Catholique Church: to the end, that a sinnefull soule, being coniunced by these sacred authorities and admonitions; may by the instinct of the holy Ghost, be conuerted (as a sheepe that was perished and lost) to Christ Iesus the Pastor and Bishop of our soules, being the onely light

Eccl. 12

light of truth and iuftice: and acknow-
ledging the wretched ftate, danger,
errours, and vncleannes, wherein
hitherto shee hath liued, may by inward sorrow and compunction conuert her selfe to God: and being conuerted doe penance, and laftly after
this short and tranfitorie life, enioy life
euerlafting with all the holy Angells
and Sainkts.

Certainely as S. Iohn Chryfoftome
doth affirme, now is the time that
vanitie of vanities doth delude the hearts
of mortal men. And therefore thofe
that liue amidft worldly pleafures and
riches, ought to write this fentence
vpon their walls, to haue it embro-
dered on their garments, to haue it en-
grauen on the dores and fore-fronts
of their houfes, but aboue all in their
confciences; to the end they may
alwayes haue the fame before their
eies, and feele it in their hearts.
And for that there are many toyes and
foolish reprefentations, which deceiue
fuch as are carelefle:it were verie good
daily to recite this verfe at dinner and
at fupper, and in all affemblies: willingly

lingly to heare others, and to sing our selues: *Vanitas vanitatum, & omnia vanitas*: that is to say, *Vanitie of vanities, and all things vanitie*. For all things passe away besides the loue of God, and his seruice onely. Thus S. Chrysostome.

Howbeit this present Treatise doth containe seuen Chapters according to the dayes of the weeke: to the end that a sinnefull soule being defiled with sinne, may euerie day take a particular Chapter, as a new mirrour or looking glasse, wherein to behold her face. The first shall be of the basenesse and miserie of man. The second of sinne in generall: and the great domage that it bringeth vnto the soule. The third of speedily doing penance. The fourth of flying and contemning the world. The fift of despising all transitorie riches, dignities, honours, and honourable offices. The sixt of the continual feare, which we ought to haue of death. The seuenth and last of the ioyes of heauen, and paines of hell.

P   CHAP.

CHAPTER I.

Of the basenesse , and miserie of man.

THe Prophet Ieremie considering the miserie of man, brake forth into these dolefull wordes following: Iere.20. *Why came I (saith he) out of the wombe, that I should see labour and sorrow, and my dayes should be spent in confusion?* If he speake thus of himselfe , whome God sanctified in his mothers wombe: what shall I say of my selfe, whome my mother conceiued in sinne? S. Bernard likewise doth exhort vs saying: Studie to know thy selfe ; because thou art farre more better, and more laudable, if thou know thy selfe , then if neglecting thy selfe, thou didst know the course of the starres, the vertue of hearbs , the complexions of men, the natures of beasts , and hadst all knowledge of heauenly and earthly things.

Con-

Confider ô man what thou haft beene before thy birth ; and what thou art from thy birth vntill thy death ; and what thou shalt he after this life. Certainely thou haft beene that which thou waft not: afterwards , being formed of vile matter and enuelopped in moft bafe attaire, thou haft beene nourished in thy mothers wombe with menftrued blood , and thy beft coate was but the skinne called *fecundina.* Thus clothed and adorned , thou haft come vnto vs ; neither doft thou remember now how bafe thy beginning is.

Forme , *youthfull heate,* Wealth , *popularitie,*
Haue *made thee fenfelffe of mortalitie.*

For man is nothing els , but filthy feede , a fack of dung , and meate for wormes.

Like paft, Wormes *come, ftench, horrour doth enfue:*
Mans *made no man : this for our guilt is due.*

Why therefore art thou proud ô man, confidering that thou haft beene vile feede , and blood curded in thy

mothers

mothers wombe? Next expofed to the
miferies of this life, and to finne; and
laftly to be wormes meate lying in
thy tōbe. Why doft thow grow proud,
ô duft and ashes; whofe conception is
finne, birth miferie, life paine, death
anguish? Whereof is mā proud, whofe
conception is finne, birth paine, life
labour, death of neceffitie?

Sen. 2.   *God therefore framed man of the slyme of*
the earth: which is the bafeft of all the
elements. God hath framed the pla-
netts and ftarres of the nature and par-
ticipation of fire: the windes and birdes of the ayre: the fishes of the water;
bnt men and beafts he made of the
earth. If therefore thou confider the
creature compofed of the water, thou
wilt find thy felfe bafe: if thou confider
thofe of the ayre, thy bafenes is yet
more: but if thou reflect vpon thofe
that are forme d of fire, thou wilt find
thy felfe to be a moft bafe creature:
being neither able to cōpare thy felfe
to thofe that are celeftial, nor da-
ring to preferre thy felfe before thofe
that are terreftriall. But if thou wilt
needes make comparifiō, let it be with
                                    brute

brute beastes void of reason, and thou wilt find thy selfe most like vnto thé, and of the same condition. For as the wise man saieth: *There is one death of man* Eccle. 3 *and beastes , and the condition of both is equall: as má dieth, so they also die: all things breath alike: and man hath nothing more then a beast: all things are subiect to vanitie , and all things passe to one place: of earth they were made, and into earth they returne toge-ther.*

If thou desire yet more plainely to heare what thou art according to thy humane nature, listen to that starre of doctors S. Augustine , speaking after this manner : Ah , (alas wretch) what am I ? I am a vessel of filthines, a receptacle of rottennes , full of horrour and and stench: blind, poore, naked, and subiect to many miseries : knowing neither my entring into the world, nor my going forth : being wretched and mortal: whose dayes passe away as a shadow : whose life changeth as the moone , florisheth and fadeth like the leafe of a tree : finally I am a clot of earth, full of wretchednes, the sonne of wrath, a vessull apt to containe contumelies:

melies: begotten in vncleannes, liuing in miserie, and shortly to die in anguish.

To the like effect writeth that most blessed Doctor S. Bernard. The flesh (saieth he) to which the soule is linked in such a great league of amitie, is nothing els but a certaine froath made flesh, clothed with a brickle beautie: but the time will come, when it will be a miserable and rotten carkasse, and foode for wormes. For albeit it be pampered neuer so much, yet it is still flesh. If thou diligently consider what doth issue forth by thy mouth, nostrills, and other passages or pores of thy bodie, thou must needes confesse, that thou neuer sawest any dung-hill more loathsome and filthy.

Of the same matter Pope Innocentius likewise writeth thus: O vile indignitie of mans condition! Consider the hearbes and trees. They of their owne accord bring forth leaues, flowers, and fruit: and thou of thy selfe bringest forth, neetes, lice, and maggots. They of themselues produce wine, oyle, and baulme, and thou of

thy

thy felfe produceft fpittle, vrine, and dung. They of themfelues breath forth a moft fweete fmell and odour, and thou fendeft forth a moft abominable fent and fauour. According as the tree is, fuch is the fruit: for a bad tree cannot bring forth good fruit.

Now tell me (I pray thee) what other thing is man, fauing a tree turned vpfide downe? whofe roote is the haire: whofe trunk is the head and neck: whofe ftock is the breaft and armeholes: whofe boughes or branches are the armes and thighes: whofe leaues are the fingers and ioynts: and to fay *Iob. 13.* the truth, man is a leafe, that is violently toffed to and fro with the wind: & ftubble, that is dried with the funne. And therefore Iob faieth moft truly of him: *Man borne of a Woman, liuing a* *Iob. 14.* *short time, is replenished with many miferies:* *Who as a flower commeth forth, and is de-* *ftroyed, and flieth as a shadow, and neuer* *abideth in the fame ftate.* For this caufe likewife God faieth to man in the third of Genefis: *Duft thou art, and into duft* *Gen. 3.* *thou shalt returne.* And Iob reciprocally faieth to God: *Remember I befeech thee,* *Iob. 10.*

that

that as clay thou madest me, and into dust
thou wilt bring me againe:

Why therefore art thou proud ô
slyme of the earth ? why dost thou
pamper thy flesh with daintie fare,
and adorne it with rich attire , which
after a few dayes the wormes are to
deuour in thy sepulcher ? and dost not
rather adorne thy soule with good
workes, which is to be presented in
heauen before God and his Angells?
Why dost thou make so small account
of thy soule, and preferre thy flesh before the same ? The maistresse to be
made the maide, and the maide the
maistresse is a great abuse.

O soule of man, thou hast a dome-
stical enemie, a friend that is thine ad-
uersarie ; that rendreth euill for good,
and vnder the colour of friendship,
doeth thee all the mischeefe that can
be deuiced. This fained friend of thine
(ô soule of man) is thy flesh , which
thou louest so much : this when thou
hast fed , thou hast raised vp a foe
against thee;this when thou hast adorned , thou hast armed an enemie : this
when thou hast clothed in furres and
rich

rich array, thou hast bereaued thy self
of the heauenly ornaments of vertue.
Consider ô sinnefull man what thou
shalt be after this life : certainely thou
wilt be a loathsome and rotté carcasse,
and meat for wormes.

Tell me (saieth S. Bernard) where
are the louers of this world, who not
long since liued and conuersed heere
on earth with vs? There is nothing remaining of them, but ashes and wormes. Weigh diligently what they are,
and what they were. They were mē, as
thou art; they did eate, drîke ād laughe
They lead their dayes in Wealth, and in a Iob. 21.
moment they are gone do Wne to hell. Heere
their flesh is adiudged to the wormes,
and there their soule to euerlasting
tormenrs; vntill being vnited together
againe, they be ouerwhelmed in perpetual paine, that haue beene companions together in sinne. For it is meete
that they be linked together in tormēt
that so louingly liued together in pleasure and coutentment.

What doth vaine glorie, transitorie
mirth, worldly power, carnal pleasure,
false riches, a great familie, and euill

Q   concu-

concupifcence now auaile them?
Where is their laughing, where is their
recreation, where istheir pride, where
is their boafting? Of fo great ioy, how
great forrow doth enfue. After a little
pleafure , how greiuous miferie doth
follow? After a few trâfitorie pleafures
and contentments, they are fallen into
endleffe miferie , deftruction, and torments. Whatfoeuer hath hapned to
them , may happen to thee , for that
thou art a man : a man made of earth,
flyme of flyme. Thou art of the earth,
and liueft of the earth, ãd shalt returne
into earth , when that laft day
shall come , which commeth on a fodaine , and perchance will be to day.
That thou shalt die is a thing moft
certaine and fure: but vncertaine whê,
or how, or where. And for that death
expecteth thee euerie where: thou
likewife, if thou be wife, wilt expect
the fame euerie where. Thus S. Bernard.

Ifidorus alfo writeth thus of the louers of this world: Moft deare brethren,
we ought to côfider how short the felicitie of this world is, ãd how the glorie

rie thereof is little: the temporal pompe and power fleeting and fraile : Tell me (he that can) where are now the Kings, where are the Princes, Emperours, ãd other potétates of the world? They are passed away as a shadow, and vanished away as a dreame: if you seeke them, they are not to be foúd. What shall I say more? Both Kings and Princes are dead and gone : howbeit many of them thought that they should liue long , and behaued themselues in that manner as if they should haue remained heere for euer. Not *so* , ô *you Wicked, not so: but you shall die like men, and fall like one of the Princes.*

Wisd. 5

Psal. 2.
Psal. 31.

S. Bernard speaking of the state or condition of man after death, vseth these wordes: What is more filthy and stinking then the dead carcasse of a man? What is more gastly to looke vpon? He whose embracements where most pleasing, whiles he liued: doth with his verie sight, affright the beholders, after he is dead. What then do riches profit vs? What do pleasures , or honoures auaile vs? Riches doe not free a man from death , nor pleasures

Q 2 from

from wormes, nor honoures from ill
fauoures or ftenches.

S. Iohn Chryfoftome likewife to the
fame effect writeth thus : What doth it
profit them, that haue perfeuered in
luxurie, and other earthly pleafures to
the verie laft day of their liues? Caft
thine eies now vpon their graues, and
fee, if there be any figne left of their
boafting : marke whether thou canft
perceiue any tokens of their riches or
lafciuioufnes : aske, what is now become of their braue apparail ád ornaments ? Where is now the pleafures of
their pageants, and other corporal có-
tentméts? Where are now their guefts,
and troupes of attendants? Their fea-
fting, laughing, fporting, ád immode-
rate mirth is at an end. All are now gone, both the maifters and their men,
and no man knoweth what is become
of them. Behold what the éd is of both
of them : looke diligently into their
fepulchers, ád thou shalt find nothing
but ashes, and the loathfome reliques
of wormes : and remember that
this is or will be the end of thy deareft
friends and acquaintance: whether
they

they passe ouer their liues in mirth and pleasures, or in labour, and abstinence. Would to God thou wouldst carefully consider and meditate on these things.

But alas the vnhappie children of Adā, leauing the true and wholesome studies of matters belonging to their saluation? seeke rather after earthly and transitorie things. Howbeit I would wish thee (deare Christian brother) to ruminate in thine heart vpon thine owne basenes and miserie, according to thine outward man follow ād affect humilitie: shunne pride and hautines, knowing that this is the signe, by which the diuel doth distinguish those that are his from others. Wherevpon Iob in his 41. Chapter affirmeth, saying: *He is King ouer all the children of* Iob 41. *pride.*

S. Gregorie doth auouch the same. Pride, sayeth he, is a most pregnant signe of the reprobate, humilitie of the elect. And by these two signes (as by two distinct colours) we know vnder what king or captaine euerie mā fighteth; to wit, Christ or the diuel. Heere

vpon

vpon Ifidorus faieth : the foule of a
proud man is forfaken by God , and
made the dwelling place of the diuells.
The Preacher doth confirme this, in
one of his fermons , faying : *Pride is*
Eccl. 10 *odious before God and men* . As by
many examples may be plainely feene.
For pride caft Lucifer out of heauen,
droue Adam out of paradife: drowned
Pharao and his armie: depriued Saul of
his kingdome: changed Nabuchodo-
nozer into a beaft : for pride Antio-
chus died of a difeafe moft loathfome
and abominable, and Herod was ftroo-
ken by an Angel.

CHAPTER II.

*Of finne in general: and the great domage
that it bringeth vnto the foule.*

H E *that committeth finne (* fayeth
1.Io.3.   S. Iohn : *) is of the diuel : becaufe the diuel finneth from the beginning.* Sinne is fuch a burden , that heauen could not fuftaine the fame, ád laftly

ly the earth will not suftaine it, but it shall descend into hell with him that committeth it. And we are to know, that according to S. Auguftine, euerie word, deede, or desire contrarie to the law of God is a sinne: which euerie one that defireth to be saued, ought with great diligence to auoid. And this efpicially for three reasons. Firft for that it is verie hatefull in the fight of God. Secondly for that it is verie delightfull to the diuells. Thirdly for that it is verie hurtfull vnto man.

I told thee firft ô man that thou oughteft with great diligence to efchew all finne, for that it is verie hatefull in the fight of God thy Creator. And that thou maieft fee this the better, call to mind, what God hath done through the hatred of finne. Firft therefore through his hatred to finne he deftroyed almoft all his workes, to wit the whole world by the general deluge as is recorded in the feuenth of Genefis. Other Kings and Princes to the preiudice of their enemies do waft and fpoile their enemies countries: but God fpoiled his owne countrie (to wit
the

the earth) for that finne had entred into it.

Moreouer God doth not onely hate finne, but likewife whatioeuer is touched with the fame. Other men, when their wine is corrupted, do not caft their golden or filuer veffells into the fea, in which it was contained: but keepe the veffell, and throw away the wine: but God (to shew his hatreo to finne) will not onely caft finne, but alfo reafonable creatures which are the veffells of finne (to wit mens foules created according to his owne image, and redeemed with his owne moft pretious blood) into the bottomleffe fea of perditiō. And therefore the wife man faieth: *To God the impious and his impietie are odious alike.* In fo much that God hath not any friend either in heauen or in earth, (albeit he loue him neuer fo dearely) whome he would not hate mortally, if he should find in him but one mortall finne onely: fo that S. Peeter himfelfe had beene damned (although he loued our Sauiour more arcently then the reft of the Apoftles) if he had died after he had denied

Wif. 14

nied our Lord thrice, without repentance.

Secondly it appeareth how much God doth detest sinne, in that for the sinne of the world he killed his innocent and onely begotten sonne, like as he testifieth by the prophet Isay, saying: *For the wickednes of my people I haue striken him.* Yea the sonne of God himselfe, that he might destroy and kill sinne, deliuered his soule vnto death, as is auouched in the same place. Now what man is there, that hateth his enemie so much, that in hatred of him, he would kill his owne sonne? Isai. 53.

Thirdly this thing is euidētly seene, for that God hath persecuted sinne from the beginning: in so much that he hath cast the same out of heauen: ād seeing that it yet remained on earth, to wit in the world, he descended into the world in his owne person, that he might chase sinne out of the same: and finally at the day of iudgement he will chase the same away for good and all, and shut it vp for euer in the darke prison of hell. Which caused the prophet Micheas to say: *He will cast all our sinnes* Mich. 7 *into* R o *into the bottome of the sea.*

Fourthly Gods exceeding great hatred to sinne, appeareth plainely by this similitude ensuing. A good mother should seeme to hate that verie much, for which shee should put her child into a fierie fournace, and should neuer draw him out from thence: so God through his hatred to sinne, will cast his children into vnquencheable fire, if he find them guiltie after death but of one mortal sinne, whome neuer. theleffe he hath loued so dearely, as that he hath vouchsafed to die for the.

Thus therefore, ô sinnefull soule, thou haft read and seene, how much God doth abhorre sinne: wherefore if thou desire to please him, seeke aboue all things to eschew sinne, and do not permit it by any meanes to abyde in thy conscience. That woman should shew her selfe verie disloyall to her husband, that should harbour a man in her bed, whome her husband hated, and by whome many hurts and harms had hapned to her husband: sinne is the thing, which Christ the celestial bridegroome of our soules doth so much deteft,

deteſt, and for which he hath endured
ſo many miſeries and afflictions, and
laſtly death it ſelfe. Whererefore deare
Chriſtian brother, I earneſtly exhort
thee to flie ſinne, and to follow the example of the Prophet Dauid, crauing
Gods aſſiſtance to auoid the ſame, and
ſaying: *Create a cleane heart in me, lô God,* Pſal. 50
and renew a right ſpirit in my boWells. &c.

Secondly thou oughteſt with great
care and diligence to eſchew ſinne eſpecially mortal, for that it is moſt pleaſing the diuell, and dilighteth him a-
boue all other things: which thou may-
eſt eaſily perceiue by theſe three ſig-
nes or tokens. The firſt is, that the diuel
ſeeketh no other ſolace: neither ſiluer,
nor gold, nor any temporal riches, but
onely mens ſoules: Wherevpon Barra
king of Sodome, in the fourteenth
Chapter of Geneſis ſpeaking to Abraham, ſaieth figuratiuely in his perſon:
Giue me the ſoules, the reſt take to thee. And Gen. 14
S.Gregorie writing vpô the ſame place,
ſaieth : That the diuel thinketh that
he hath done nothing, vntill he haue
wounded the ſoule with the dart of
mortal ſinne: For like as a hauke or
faulcon

R 2

faulcon especially desireth the heart of the bird that it seizeth vpon : so the diuel doth chiefely couet the soule of a man.

The second signe that the diuel loueth sinne, is his cōtinual temptatiō and soliciting of men to the same, and for that he is neuer wearie of committing sinne. For he hath now cōmitted sinne sixe thousand yeares and more, and yet he is as readie to procure new offeces as euer he was heretofore. Whervpon it is written in the first of Iob, that when our Lord asked him, saying: *Whence commest thou? He answering, said: I haue gone round about the earth, and walked through it.* Yea he is so busied in inciting men to sinne, that he hath no list to sleepe, according to that of Iob: *They that eate me, sleepe not.*

The third signe that sinne doth verie much delight the diuel, is, that he could neuer be yet satiated with sinne: for albeit he hath alreadie deuoured infinite millions of men for sinne, yet he is still hungrie and desireth more: *And as a roaring lion goeth about seeking whome he may deuoure,* as S.Peter testifieth

Iob 1.

Iob 30.

1.Pet.5.

fieth in his firſt Epiſtle ãd fifth chapter.
Neither is he hungrie onely, but likewiſe thirſtie, and therefore Iob ſpea-
king of him, ſaieth : *He ſhall ſup vp the*   Iob 40
riuer, and ſhall not maruaile : and he hath a
confidence, that Iordan may runne into his
mouth. The riuer, which the diuel ſup-
peth vp and doth not maruaile, are ſinners, running ſwiftly into the infernal
mouth of hell : neither is he content
with this, but hopeth that Iordan (by
which are vnderſtood ſuch as are religious) will paſſe into his mouth by the
ſame water-courſe, I meane of ſinne,
and wickednes. We haue an example
of this in the liues of the ancient holy
Fathers : where it is ſaid, that one of
them was praiſed and honoured by the
prince of the diuells, and placed by
him in a chaire of ſtate : for that he had
made a Monke to commit fornication,
whome after fourtie yeares temptation, he had with much adoe induced
to ſinne.

Wherefore ô ſinnefull ſoule, lament
and be ſorrowfull : for that thou haſt
cauſed thine enemies (to wit the diuells) to reioyce ſo often ouer thee, as
thou

thou haſt ſinned mortally : and heere-after haue a care by a pure confeſſion and condigne ſatisfaction, that God and his holy Angells may reioyce ouer thee in heauen.

Thirdly thou oughteſt to eſchew ſinne with all care and diligence, for that it hurteth thee verie much : for by ſinne we are ſeparated from the loue of God, and become his enemies: This made the Prophet Iſay to ſay to the children of Iſrael : *Behold the hand of our Lord is not abridged, that he cannot ſaue; neither is his eare made heauie, that it cannot heare : but your iniquities haue deuided betweene you and your God, and your ſinnes haue hid his face from you, that he would not heare.*

Ifay 59.

Such is Gods hatred towards ſinne, that if the greateſt Sainct in heauen ſhould offend, he would preſently be caſt downe out of that happie place, and the amitie of God towards him would immediatly ceaſe. Wherevpon S. Auguſtine ſaieth : He that ſinneth againſt a moſt true and faithfull frid, is worthy to be reprehended : but he that ſinneth againſt God, his moſt po-

tent

rent and pious father, how can he be excused from deseruing to be both re-prehended and hated?

Fourthly a sinner by sinne is obliged and adiudged to the gibbet of hell: and for that the law of God in this case is not much different from the law of man, therefore all transgressors and traytors, that is to say, all sinners, de-serue to be hanged, according as is signified in the third booke of Esdras in the decree of King Darius, where he saieth thus. *And that it be denounced, that whosoeuer shall transgresse any thing of these that are written*, (that is by the sinne of commission) *or shall despise it* (to wit by the sinne of omission) *a beame be taken of their owne*, (that is out of the garden of their owne conscience, for there groweth the timber on which a sinner is to be tormented) *and they be hanged, and their goods be confiscate to the king*: for aswell the punishment of the wicked, as the reward of the good, tend to the honour and glorie of God.

Behold deare Christian brother what humane lawes effect corporally, the same doth the law of God accomplish

spiri-

3. Esdr. 6.

spiritually. The like disasterous euent
we read to haue hapned to wicked
Aman in the seuenth Chapter of the
booke of Esther, by whome we may
anagogically vnderstand a sinner:
whome the king of heauen will command to be execured on the gibbet of
eternal perdition, if he finally find him
guiltie of mortal sinne.

Fifthly sinne bereaueth a man of the
benefit of grace in this life, and of glorie in the world to come. And therefore in the Prouerbes, it is truly said,
that *sinne maketh men wretched.* For a sinner is poore, for that he hath nothing:
yea by mortal sinne he selleth himselfe,
and becometh the slaue of the diuel.
He is yet more poore, because he can
gaine nothing: for that aslong as he is
in that state, he can doe no meritorious
act, or that is gratefull to God. But he is
yet most poore, because nothing can
be giuen him: for the good workes,
that are done for him, do nothing
auaile him to saluation: because he liueth in respect of his bodie onely.

Wherevpon Boetius saieth in the
fourth booke of his Treatise intituled
the

Pro.14.

the comfort of Philofophie : A wicked
man can no otherwife be termed a má,
then as we call him that is dead, a man.
For by finne a man is feparated from
the true light of grace : he is blinded,
and ouerwhelmed with darknes. The
Prophet Sophonias teftifieth the fame,
faying : *They shall walke as blind-men,* Sopho.
becaufe they haue finned to our Lord. And 1.
in the pfalme : *They knew not, neither*
did they vnderftand, they walke in darke- Pfal.81.
neffe : S. Hierom likewife fpeaking of
finne, hath this faying : The foule by
finne is wholy depreffed, and inwardly polluted, fo that shee is vnable to
looke vpward.

Sinne in the foule is like rottennes
in an apple : for like as rottennes in an
apple taketh away his valew, colour,
and fauour : fo finne in the foule taketh
away the valew of fame ád glorie, the
colour of beautie, and the fauour of
grace. Thus then you fee that all finne
is a certaine rottennes or putrefáctió.
Heerevpon thè wife man affirmeth of Wifd.
a finner, *That his heart is ashes, and his* 15.
hope vaine earth, and his life viler then clay.

S   S. Au-

S. Auguſtine alſo ſaieth : The ſmell
of a rotten dead dogge is more tolerable in the ſight of men, then is a ſinnefull ſoule in the ſight of God. And in a
certaine ſermon which he made to
withdraw a certaine ſinnefull man
from his lewd and wicked conuerſa-
tion , he vſeth theſe wordes: What a-
uaileth a coffer full of treaſure and riches, if the cóſcience be void of goodnes ? Wilt thou haue goods, and wilt
thou not be good thy ſelfe ? Art thou
not aſhamed , that thy houſe is full of
goods , and thou thy ſelfe art bad ? But
tell me, I pray thee , What wouldeſt
thou be content to haue bad? Nothing
at all. Not a bad wife, not a bad ſonne,
not a bad ſeruant, not a bad handmaid
not a bad coate or iacket ; laſtly not a
bad paire of breeches: and yet thou art
content to haue a bad life. Let me en-
treate thee to preferre thy life at leſt
before thy breeches. Thou lookeſt
round about thee vpó thine apparaile,
and likeſt all well (all being braue
and beautifull) and yet to thy ſelfe
thou art vile and abominable. If thy
goods, with which thy houſe is ſtuffed
                                        full,

fall, were able to speake vnto thee,
doubtlesse they would say: Thou desirest to haue vs good, we likewise do
desire to haue a good maister or Lord:
and by their crie they call vpon God
against thee. Behold, (say they to God)
thou hast giuen this man so great store
of goods, and yet he is bad: what doth
it profit him to haue all these things,
sithence he hath not him, that hath giuen him all these things?

Sixthly by sinne, a man becommeth
like vnto a bruit beast, void of reason.
Wherevpō Boetius in his fourth booke
of the comefort of Philosophie
sayeth: a vertuous man leauing vertue
is changed into a beast. And Aristotle
in his Ethickes, saieth, that he is worse
then a beast. To which agreeth that of
Dauid, saying : *Man, when he was in ho-* Psal. 48
nour, did not vnderstand : he was compared
to beasts without vnderstanding, and became
like to them.

Seuenthly and lastly by sinne a man
becommeth the child and slaue of the
diuel. Wherevpon S. Iohn saieth in his
first Epistle: *He that committeth sinne, is of* 1. Io. 3.
the diuel. Now therefore ō vnhappie

sinner, let all these motiues moue thee
to take pittie of thy soule, and do not
by sinne, be the cause of her vtter destruction, but remember the manifold
euills that haue beene heere mentio-
ued; to wit, how by sinne thou hast
offended almightie God, reioyced the
diuel, and endommaged thine owne
soule.

Acknowledge therefore ô man how
noble thy soule is, and how grieuous
the woundes thereof haue beene, for
which it was necessarie that Christ our
Lord should be slaine. If they had not
beene to death, and to death euerlasting, the sonne of God would neuer
haue died for the cure of them. Do not
therefore make small account of thy
soules passion or miserie, towards
whome thou seest so great compassion
shewed by so great a maiestie. He hath
powred forth teares for thee: do thou
likewise wash thy couch euerie night,
by compunction of heart and continual lamentation. He hath powred
forth his blood, do thou likewise powre forth thine, by daily affliction of
thy bodie. Which if thou canst not
shed

shed for Chrift at one time, at leaft
fpend it after a more mild, though after a more long martyrdome. Neuer
reflect what the flesh defireth, but
what the fpirit requireth.

For as S. Gregorie faieth: the more
that the flesh is for a time fweetly dili-
ghted:the more the fpirit is euerlafting
ly tormented: and by how much the
more the flesh is in this life afflicted by
fo much the more it shall reioyce in
eternal beatitude.

Let vs therefore now (according to
the counfel of S. Auguftine) forfake
our owne wills for the loue of Chrift
for a time, which we muft leaue at
length, though we be neuer fo vnwilling: leaft (which God forbid) for
things tranfitorie, we loofe thofe that
are euerlafting.

For if one should fay vnto thee. Take
thy pleafure as much as thou wilt,
yet with this conditio, that afterwards
thou shalt haue thine eies pulled out:or
be depriued all the reft of thy life of all
ioy and confort, yea (which is worfe)
be perpetually tormeted with hunger
and thirft and all manner of miferies
and

and punishmēts: certainely I imagine,
that thou wouldest neuer accept of
a little transitorie pleasure vpon such a
hard condition. Consider then that the
whole life of mā is not to be esteemed
as much as a moneth, or a day, or one
hower onely, in comparison of the e-
ternal miserie of the damned, which
hath neither end, neither can any
paine or torment be compared vnto it.

CHAPTER III.

Of speedily doing penance.

Mat.10.   HE that taketh not his crosse, and followeth me, is not worthy of me,
saieth our Sauiour to his disciples in
the Gospel of S. Matthew. By this
crosse is signified penance, which euerie sinner must of necessitie take vp,
and beare with perseuerance, if he desire to raigne with Christ in eternal
happines. Wherevpon S. Hierome
wri-

writing to a certaine woman named
Susanna, vseth these wordes. Penance
is necessarie and expedient; which
ought either to equalize or exceede
the sinnes which we haue committed.
S. Augustine is of the same opinion.
Whosoeuer, (saieth he) desireth to be
saued: must wash away, at least with
the internal teares of contrition whatsoeuer he hath contracted after the
puritie of baptisme.

But perchance thou wilt say. This is
a hard speech: I cannot despise the
world; neither can I hate, and chastice
mine owne flesh. Cócerning this matter heare not mine but S. Hieromes answere. It is hard, saieth he, yea impossible, that a má eioy the cómodities of
this life, and those of the life to come:
that heere he fill his bellie, and there
his mind: that he passe from delights
to delights: that he be the first in both
worldes: that he appeare glorious in
heauen, and in earth. Which sentence
cf Saint Hierome, Saint Gregorie
doth confirme, saying: Many desire to mount vp from the iustice of
this vale of teares to the ioyes of paradise,

dife, but yet they will not want their
worldy pleafures: the grace of Chrift
doth call them, but the concupifcence
of the world doth recall them: they defire to die like iuft men, but they will
not liue like vnto them: and thefe shall
perish for euer, becaufe their workes
do follow them.

S. Bernard is of the fame opinion,
who fpeaking of the auftere life of S.
Iohn Baptift, faieth thus: the aufteritie
of S. Iohn Baptifts conuerfation, is a
heauie meffenger of eternal death to
finners, that are delicious and wanton.
Whence is it, that we that are little
better the bruit beaftes void of reafon,
and wormes of the earth do grow
proud, and refufe to doe penance, fithence he, (then whome there hath
not rifen a greater amongft the children of woemen) hath fo afflicted his
moft innocent bodie? nay contrariwife
we loue to be cloathed in braue attire,
and to ftuffe our paunches with good
cheere; Not fo, ô ye wicked, not fo:
this is not the way to heauen. Finally
remember the parable or hiftorie of
the rich glutton, who was Lord of fo
                                    much

much wealth : who was cloathed Luc.16.
with silke and purple, and fared deli-
ciously euerie day: remember (I say)
how he in his greatest necessitie, when
the flames of hell fire did so exceedingly afflict him, could not obtaine so
much as a drop of cold water to coole
his tongue.

Remember these things (deare
Christiã Reader) whiles thou hast time
to doe penance. For as S. Gregorie
saieth : Although almightie God hath
promised pardõ to him that repenteth,
yet he hath not promised to morrow
to him, that sinneth. And if you desire
to know, what penance or repentance
is; It is to lament our former offences,
and not to commit, nor to haue a purpose of committing things worthy of
lamentation. Wherevpon S. Augustine
saieth in his soliloquies. That penance
is peeuish and without profit, which
is defiled by an ensuing fault. Lamentation doth but little good, if our sinnes be reiterated. It nothing auaileth
vs to aske pardon of our sinnes, if(like
a dogge to the vomit) we returne to
them againe.

T   How-

Howbeit for a more ample declaration of the premises, note that there are three principal parts of penance: to wit, contrition of heart, Confession of mouth, and satisfaction of worke. For sithence we do offend God three wayes; to wit, by delectatiō of thought by vnaduisednes of word, and by pride of worke: and sithence likewise (according to the maximé or principle of Phisitians) CONTRARIES ARE CVRED BY CONTRARIES: we make amends by three opposite wayes: that is, by opposing contrition against delectation of thought, confession against vnaduisednes of word, and satisfaction against pride of worke. And fot that I purpose to speake a word or two of each of these three principal parts of penance, I thinke it best to begin first with the first.

Contrition therefore is a sorrow voluntarily conceiued for sinne, with a purpose of abstaining, confessing, and satisfying. And according to the assertion of S. Bernard, this sorrow ought to be three fold, sharpe, sharper, and sharpest of all. It ought to be sharpe,

for

for that we haue offended our Lord
God, who is the Creator of all things.
Sharper, for that we do resist our heauenly father, who doth so liberally
feede vs: and in this we are worse then
dogges, who loue, and follow those
that feede them. Sharpest of all, for
that (as much as lieth in vs) we cruci-
fie our Redeemer againe, who hath redeemed vs with his owne blood, and
deliuered vs from the bonds of sinne,
and from the crueltie of the diuells, ād
from the bitternes of eternal damnation.

Moreouer we ought to be sorrowfull
for three things: to wit, for the sinne
which we haue committed, for the
good which we haue omitted, and for
the time which we haue idly spent and
consumed. Of the vertue and qualitie
of this contrition thus saieth that holy
Father S. Augustine : Contrition of
heart is farre better, then to goe in pilgrimage from one end of the world to
an other. Likewise a certaine glosse
vpon the psalme. Ad *Dominum cum tribu-*   Psa.119
*larer,*saieth: Our Lord cannot deferre
to pardon that man his fault, whome

T 2   he

he seeth to pray vnto him with a compunct or sorrowfull heart.

And S. Iohn Chrysostome shewing the fruits or effects of holy compunction, writeth thus: It is compunction alone, that maketh the soule to detest purple, to desire cloath of haire : to loue teares, and to loath laughter. And in an other place. Nothing doth so conglutinate and vnite to God, as the teares of a penitent. Neither can we (as S. Augustine doth auouch) giue the diuel greater cause of griefe and anguish: then when we heale the hurts of our sinnes by confession and penáce. But albeit the fruits and effects of penance, be so great, yet there are verie few (alas) that do practice it. And of this our Lord complaineth by the Prophet Ieremie, saying: *No man speaketh* *that Which is good, there is none that doth* *penance for his sinne, saying : What haue* I *done?*

Ierem:8

The second principal part of penance to wit, Confession, is wont to be described, to be a conuenient declaration of our sinnes before a Priest. For confession (according to the Etymologie

logie or true interpretation of the
vvorde) is a confessing or acknowled-
ging of our fault. For he maketh a true
confession, that confesseth or acknowledgeth whatsoeuer he hath done. Or
Confession (according as Isidorus
saieth in his booke of Etymologies)
is that, by which the secret disease of
our soule is (to the praise of God)
discouered and laid open, through
hope of obtaining pardon. Of the
vertue of vvhich S. Ambrose vpon the
psalme : *Beati immaculati*, saieth in this Psa.118
manner.Gods vengeance or furie doth
cease and can doe no more, if mans
confession goe before.And Cassiodorus
vpon the psalme : *Confiteantur tibi populi* Psal.6.
Deus, saieth thus : Christ is not a iudge,
but an aduocate to them : who haue
condemned themselues by their owne
confession. S. Leo the Pope affirmeth
the same : That remaineth not (saieth
he) to be condemned at the day of
doome, which hath beene cleansed in
confession.

S. Augustine likewise in his treatise
of penance giueth Confession this
commendation.Confession (saieth he)

is

is the faluation of foules, the deftroyer of finnes, the reftorer of vertues, the affaulter of the diuells. What more? It fhutteth the mouth of hell, it ope¬neth the gates of heauen. Wherefore deare Chriftian brother, let all thefe authorities of holy fathers before men-tioned, moue thee to doe according to the counfel of the Prophet Ifay, who

Ifay.43. faieth: *Tell if thou haue any thing, that thou maieft be iuftified.* For the confef-fion of our finnes is the beginning of iuftice.

Thou oughteft to confeffe all thy finnes entirely to a Prieft, that hath power to giue thee abfolution : how-beit thou muft beware, that thou do not confeffe one part of thy finnes onely to one Prieft, and an other part to an other : for fo neither of them would be able to giue thee abfolution.

In his med: chap. 9. Wherevpon S. Bernard faieth : He that to diuerfe Confeffors deuideth his confeffion, departeth without par-don : for it is a deteftable fiction to deuide our finnes, and fuperficially to fhaue them off, not intrinfecally to roofe them vp. And fuch receiue ex-

commu-

communication in steed of absolution, maledistion in steed of benediction. Hypocrisie commonly is the cause that men do thus deuide their confession: and for this reason they tell their greater sinnes to vnknowne Priests, and such as are lesse they care not much to disclose to some Priest of their acquaintance.

Of such men as these S. Augustine writeth thus : He that deuideth his confession, is not to be commended, for that he doth conceale to the one, and reueale to the other : which is to praise himselfe, and to tend to hypocrisie. The like saying we find in the Decretalls.

But leauing to say any more of this, let vs speake of satisfaction, which is the third principall part of penance. S. Augustine defineth the same thus. Satisfaction is to cut off the causes of sinnes, and not to giue way to their suggestions. For as S. Gregorie saieth; We do not make satisfaction by abstaining onely from sinne, vnlesse we likewise persecute our owne wills, which we loue, with opposite lamentations.

And

And as S. Iohn Chryfoſtome doth affirme : Such as the offéce hath beene, ſuch ought to be the reconciliation: be as prone to lamentation, as thou haſt beene to ſinne : ſuch as thine intention hath beene to ſinne, ſuch let thy deuotion be to doe penance for the ſame: grieuous ſinnes require grieuous lamentations. For as Euſebius the Biſhop ſaieth: We muſt not thinke a little contrition to be enough, to redeeme thoſe debts, to whome there is due an eternal death : neither is a little ſatisfaction ſufficient for thoſe euills, for which there is prepared an eternal puniſhment.

But alas many are preſently wearie of a penitential life, and looke back from the way of ſatisfaction with Lots wife. Againſt ſuch as theſe S. Bernard in a certaine ſermon writeth thus : He that perfectly feeleth the burden of ſinne, or the hurt that hapneth to his ſoule by the ſame : doth either verie little or not at all feele any corporal puniſhment or paine : neither is that labour grieuous vnto him, by which he knoweth his former faults are aboliſhed,

lished, and thofe auoided that are to
come. S. Auguftine likewife vpon the
firft pfalme hath thefe wordes: There
are many that are not ashamed to
finne, that would be ashamed to doe
penance or fatisfaction.

O incredible madnes! Art thou not
ashamed of thy wound? Is not finne a
loathfome and ftinking wound? Flie
therefore to the Phifitiã: doe penance:
fay: *I do know mine iniquitie, and my finne* Pfal. 50.
is before me alwayes. To *thee onely haue I*
finned: for that thou alone art without
finne.

Howbeit fatisfaction confifteth in
three things: vz, in prayer, fafting, and
almefdeedes: that fo a three fold remedie may be applied againft the
three fold maladie, which we fo often
full into through the malice of our
ghoftly aduerfarie: prayer againft pride: fafting againft carnal concupifcence: almefdeedes againft auarice.
Or thus: Euerie finne is either committed againft God, and againft this is
ordained prayer: or againft our neighbour, and againft this is ordained
almes-deedes: or againft our felues,

V   and

and againſt this is ordained faſting.

And for a more ample declaration
of ſatisfaction , I meane to ſay a word
or two of almeſdeedes. In Latine it is
called *Eleemoſyna* , which is deriued
from the Greeke worde *Eleemo*, which
ſignifieth mercifull , and *ſyna* , which
ſignifieth a commandement , as if we
should ſay , the commandement of
mercie. And in this ſenſe it is to be
written with an e. It is wont likewiſe
to be written with a y , and then it is
aſmuch as if you should ſay , the commandement of God. For he by his
owne mouth hath commanded it to
Luc. 11. be done. *Giue almes* (ſaieth he) *and behold*
all things are cleane vnto you. Or other-
wiſe the word *Eleemoſyna* (ſignifying
almes) is deriued from *Ely* , which is
God, and *moys* water : as if we should
Eccli. 3. ſay , the water of God. For as *Water*
quencheth burning fire : ſo almes reſiſteth
ſinnes.

Howbeit there are three things eſpecially, which ought to incite vs to giue
almes , and to doe other workes of
mercie. The firſt is , for that mercie
doth redeeme ſinne. Of this the wiſe
man

man doth assure vs in his prouerbes,
saying : *By mercie and truth iniquitie is* Pro.16.
redeemed. Daniel likewise gaue this
counsel to Nabuchodonosor : to wit, Dan.4.
that he should redeeme his sinnes
with almes, and his iniquities with the
mercies of the poore. We read in the
fourth booke of Kings, that a certaine 4. King.
poore widow being in distresse came 4.
to the Prophet Elizeus , crauing his
assistance : who bad her borrow many
emptie vessells of her neighbours, and
to power part of a little oyle , which
shee had yet remaining, into each one
of them: which shee doing, the vessells
became all full , and that in such
aboundant manner , as that shee
had where withall both to maintaine
her selfe and her children , and to
pay her creditour . By these emptie,
vessells are vnderstood the poore
whome we ought to harbour in our
houses according as our Lord by the
mouth of the Prophet Isay willeth vs.
Breake thy bread (saieth he) *to the hun-*
grie, and the needie, ād the harbourlesse bring Isay. 58
into thin thouse. The little oyle which
we ought to powre into euerie vessell,

V 2   is

is our temporal substance , whereof we must giue almes , as much as our meanes will permit vs : according to the counsell of old Tobias. *If thou haue much*, saieth he, *giue abundantly : if thou haue little, studie also to impart a little willingly.* Then the oyle of mercie is said to encrease , when a sinnefull soule by merit and grace doth make satisfactió to God her creditour , for her sinnes and offenses.

Tob. 4.

Secondly by almes-deedes our temporall goods are encreased. Wherevpő S. Gregorie saieth in his Dialogues. Our earthly riches, by this that they are giuen to the poore , are multiplied and encrease more and more. Of this we haue an exáple in the third booke of Kings and seuenteenth chapter , in the widow of Sareptha, that fed Elias: whose meale and oyle our Lord multiplied, in respect of her charitie towardes his Prophet. By which we are giuen to vnderstand , that the poore do rather feede their benefactors, then they them.

3. King. 17.

Thirdly almes-deedes or workes of mercie do gard an almes-giuer at the

the hower of death in that laſt extremitie , and conduct his ſoule with
brightnes to eternal felicitie. Where-
vpón S. Ambroſe ſaieth: Mercie alone
is the companion of thoſe that are departed. O what a good and neceſſarie
companion are almes-deedes to thoſe
that are dying! Do not therefore diſmiſſe ſuch a ſeruant , or leaue ſuch an
aduocate behind thee : as they doe,
who hoarding vp their riches , giue
nothing to the poore during their
whole life with their owne hãds, being
like to him, that will haue a candle carried behind him. The wiſe man giueth
thee better counſell, ſaying: *Say not to*
thy friend: goe, and returne: and to moto̅ w I
will giue to thee: Whereas thou maieſt giue
forthwith. Prou. 3.

Wherefore we muſt vnderſtand, that
a rich man , of whome an almes is demanded , ought to conſider two
things. Firſt, who it is, that asketh the
ſame , to wit God himſelfe , who ſo
dearely loueth the poore, that whatſoeuer thou doſt doe to the poore for
his ſake , he eſteemeth it as done to
himſelfe. For ſo he auoucheth in the
Goſpel

Mat.26 Gospel of S. Matthew: Amen I *say to you, as long as you did it to one of these my least brethren, you did it to me.* Our Lord therefore asketh an almes by the mouth of a poore man, of whome a rich man in his daily prayer asketh a kingdome. Whensoeuer a rich man therefore doth denie an almes to a poore man, he ought to feare, that God will not heare him, when he demandeth of him the kingdome of heauen. Salomon in his Prouerbes saieth

Prou.21 absolutely that he will not. *He that stoppeth his eare (saieth he) at the crie of the poore: he himselfe also shall crie and shall not be heard.*

Secondly a rich man ought to consider, what God demandeth, when he asketh an almes by the mouth of the poore: to wit, not that, which is ours, but his owne: and therefore he sheweth himselfe verie vngratefull to God, that denieth an almes to one that is in need, sithence his plentie proceedeth from God's liberalitie. And this King Dauid considered when he said to God.

1. Paralip.29. *Al things are thine (ô Lord) and things that we haue receiued of thy hand, we haue*
giuen

given thee. Verily God asketh of vs by the poore; not that we should giue, but lend: lend I say to God, which shall vndoubtedly be repaid. not two or three fold onely, but an hūdred fold. Wherevpon S. Augustine saieth: O man, why dost thou put out thy money to vse vnto men? lend it out rather vnto God, and thou shalt receiue an hundred-fold gaine, and possesse life euerlasting. He therefore is vngratefull, that will not lend his money vnto God vpon the same condition, that he would to a Iew or Sarracin.

Wherefore let these reasons and considerations (deare Christian brother) moue thee to gather together the poore, and in them to lay vp treasure before hand for thy selfe in heauen, as the securest place of all : *Where neither the rust, nor mothe doth corrupt, and where theeues do not digge through nor steale.* Mat. 6. The heart of a couetous man, is like a pit without bottome : and the more it receiueth, the more it desireth; in so much that it seemeth neuer to be full. According to that of Ecclesiastes : *A couetous mā will not be filled with money.* Eccle. 5

Moreo-

Moreouer confider, that the heart followeth the treafure, as our Sauiour teftifieth in the afore mentioned place **Mat. 6** of S. Matthew : *Where thy treafure is, there is thy heart alfo.*

And therefore woe be to him, that heapeth vp treafure on earth; for he perfecuteth his owne foule, and putteth it in danger of damnation. Whereupon S. Iohn Chryfoftome faieth: Gather thy fubftance thither, where thou haft a countrie : for he that placeth his treafure on earth, can hope for nothing in heauen : for how can he hope to receiue any thing in heauen, that hath layed vp nothing? Efteeme that to be thine onely, which thou haft beftowed vpon the poore and needie. For they are not the goods of a man, which he cannot beare with him. S. Ambrofe likewife fpeaking of almesdeedes, giueth it this commendation-There is nothing (faieth he) fo praifeworthy, as the compaffion of charitie. I do not remember that I euer read of any one that died amiffe, that willingly practiced workes of pittie towards fuch as were in diftreffe.

S. Leo

S. Leo (though in other wordes) saieth the same in effect. He sendeth the entire fruits (saieth he) to our Lord before hand, from whome the poore neuer departed sorrowfull or discontented. So great is the vertue of mercie, that other vertues without it (if there be any, where charitie the chiefe of all others is wanting) can auaile a man nothing. For albeit a man be faithfull, humble, chast, and sober, and endewed with many other rare vertues : yet if he be not mercifull towards such as are in neede, he will neuer find mercie at the hands of God.

Thus much I haue said of the vertues of almes-deedes and other workes of mercie, in fauour of such as are poore and needie. Now let vs returne to our former purpose, by speaking more at large of the vertue of penance. *He that* Mat.10. *taketh not his crosse* (saieth our Sauiour) *and followeth me, is not worthy of me.* This is the crosse of penance, which we must take vp in our young yeares, and with speede; for by this meanes it doth a man most good, and is most pleasing

X   to

to God. According to that of Ecclesia-

Eccl.12.
stes : *Remember thy Creator in the dayes of thy youth.* And in an other place the

Eccli.5.
same author saieth : *Slack not to be conuerted to our Lord, and defferre not from day to day. For his Wrath shall come sodainly, and in the time of vengeance he Will destroy thee.*

But contrarie to this wholesome counsel of the wise man, the diuel giueth a man hope of longer life, saying: Thou art yet young and strong, and likely to liue long : heereafter when thou art old, doe penāce in Gods name, and goe to confession. Many (alas) are too too light, in giuing ouer much credit to this infernal aduocate, promising them lōg life: and so deferre their amendment, with a purpose to doe it whē they are old: whome sodaine death cōmeth, and taketh away with him vnprouided, and so (poore soules) they are damned. This made the wise man

Eccl.29.
most wisely to say : *Naughtie suertiship hath vndone many.*

Wherefore we must note, that this suertiship or false assurance of the diuel concerning long life, and repentance

tance when we are old, is naught, because contrarie to right and reason:
more naught, because contrarie to 2
sinners good and saluation : most
naught, because contrarie to Gods
goodnes and compassion.

That it is naught, and contrarie to
right and reason, appeareth by these
three examples following. The first is,
that as he that hauing fower asses,
should lay the whole burden vpon the
weakest of the fower, should doe contrarie to right and reason : so he that
will impose the whole burden of the
penance due to his sinnes, which he
hath committed in his fower ages (to
wit, whiles he was a stripling, a youth,
a man of perfect groweth, and an old
man) vpon his old age onely, being
now growne weake and infirme, and
vnable to take paine. Such as these de-
serue the malediction or curse mentioned in the Prophet Malachias :
Cursed is the deceitfull, (saieth he) *that*   Mala.1.
hath in his flock a male ; and making a
vow, immolateth the feeble to our Lord:
for thus doeth he, who hauing spēt his
strong and youthfull yeares in plea-

sures and vanitie, doth purpose to offer the weakenes of his old age, as a sacrifice to God almightie. But what saieth Isidorus to such good fellowes as these? He that looseth the time that is fit for penance, cometh in vaine to Gods gate with prayers.

The second example is. He that could not lift vp a lesser burden, when he was much more strong and potent: and yet would attempt to lift it vp, whé it was become much more great, and he growne much more weake: might well be esteemed to haue neither sense nor wit: thus it fareth with him, that will not beare the burden of his sinnes and of penance, when it is lesser, and he stronger, to wit in his youth: and thinketh that he shall be able to carrie it better, when it is growne greater. Such a one is like to that foole mentioned in the liues of the fathers, that did cut woode, and made thereof a burden, and afterward tried to lift it vp: and when he saw that he was not able easily to beare the same, he went and cut more woode, and put it to his burden, and then tried
                                                again:

againe: and the more heauie it wei-
ghed, the more woode he added: Thus
doe sinners, who for a while take vp
the burden of their sinnes by doing
penance: and then feeling it somewhat
heauie and burdensome, cast it downe
againe, and adde sinne to sinne.

The third example is, that he that
during his whole life, should with
great cost and charges prepare a house
for himselfe, where he intended not to
dwell by any meanes; and should (as
much as lieth in his power) destroy
that house, where he wished and desired to abide for euer: should question-
lesse doe partly contrary to reason, and
might well be accounted a foole or a
mad man : and yet this is the proceeding of a sinner, who deferreth his
conuersiō vntill the last hower; for he,
during his whole life, prepareth his
house in hell, where notwithstanding
he would not willingly by any meanes
dwell. Wherefore he hath iust reason
to feare that dreadfull saying of Saint
Augustine : He that doeth against his
conscience, buildeth to his owne damnation.

X 3   Secon-

Secondly that this promise of longer life is yet more naught, and contrarie to a sinners good and saluation, it appeareth by these two examples ensuing. The first is, that he that should desire to be rather sick then well, to be rather a slaue then free, to be rather poore and needie, thē to abound with all manner of riches, may well be esteemed wicked, and an enemie to himselfe. Yet such a one is a sinner, that deferreth to doe penance, because he desireth rather to liue in sinne, (which is a spiritual sicknes, or rather death it selfe) then to be well, by liuing pure from the same. Or a sinner is wicked against himselfe, for that he rather desireth to be dead, then aliue, a slaue then free, euill then good. Wherevpon our Sauiour saieth in the Gospel of S. Iohn: *Euerie one which committeth sinne, is the seruant of sinne.* S. Augustine likewise confirmeth the same, saying: **A** good man albeit he serue, is free: but a bad man, albeit he raigne, is a bondman or slaue: neither of one man onely, but (which is worse) of as many maisters, as vices.

Io: 8.
S. Aug.
de ciuit.
Dei c.3.

The

The second example is this. He that should owe a great somme of money for vse or interest, which should daily encreafe : in fo much that he were hardly able to pay it, and yet he would delay, afmuch as he could : fuch a one doubtleffe should doe againft himfelfe. The like hapneth in this cafe : To remaine in finne, is to augment the fumme : becaufe the longer we linger in finne, the greater muft be our paiment of paine. For fo S. Iohn affirmeth in the Apocalyps, faying : *As much as fhee (to wit, a foule indebted to God for finne) hath glorified her felfe, and hath beene in delicacies, fo much giue her torment and mourning.* Apo. 18.

Thirdly that this promife of longer life is moft naught, and contrarie to Gods goodnes, is moft euident likewife by three examples. The firft is, if fome young man should oppofe himfelfe during his whole life againft his Lord and maifter, whome he were bound to ferue, and from whome he had all that he hath, and should ferue his maifters mortal enemie ; and afterwards being growne old and decrepit, would

would forsooth serue his true Lord and maister, and should offer him his seruice; such a one should shew himselfe to be a lewd varlet, and it is verie likely, that his seruice would be little acceptable to his Lord. Thus it fareth with a sinner, who by sinning offendeth God, and serueth his enemie the diuel in his youth, and purposeth to serue God in his old age.

The second example is this. Suppose that a seruant had receiued a great summe of money from his Lord and maister, with intent that he should multiplie and augment the same, and he contrarily should lewdly and lauishly spend it, without returning his maister any profit: such a one doubtlesse should behaue himselfe amisse, and should shew himselfe vngratefull by thus abusing his Lords courtesie and kindnes. Yet this is the case and carriage of a sinner, who hath receiued a bodie and soule with their seueral powers and forces, temporal goods, space of life, and many other great benefits from almightie God his good Lord and maister.

ster, all which by sinning, and speedily
doing amisse , he mispendeth to the
discredit and disgrace of Gods most
gratious goodnes. For of our soule,
which hath beene giuen vs by God as a
most pretious treasure, Saint Gregorie
speaketh in this manner : Woe be to
me if I negligently keepe the talent
deliuered to my charge , to wit my
soule, which hath beene prized worth
the blood of the immaculate lambe of
God. Of the time likewise which God
hath lent vs to be employed in workes
of penance (which neuerthelesse is by
most men spent amisse) the same Saint
Gregorie saieth thus. There is not so
much as a moment of time lent thee,
whereof a reckonning will not be demanded, how it hath beene spent.

The third example is. If a seruant
that were steward, or dispenser of the
goods of some great Lord, should giue
good bread , and good wine, and the
best victualls vnto strangers, and such
as were his Lords enemies : but to his
Lord and maister should giue bread
that were vinowed, or made of branne,
flesh or fish that did stinke for want of

drei-

dressing, or for hauing beene kept ouer
long ; or wine that were onely the
dreggs and bottome of a barell , or
growne so sower, that it were worth
nothing: such a one doubtlesse had iust
reason to feare his Lords fürie and indignation. And yet this is the case of a
sinner, who giueth the best part of his
life, (to wit his youth and strength) to
the world and diuel,which are the enemies of Christ : and purposeth to giue
the worst and last of his life to God.
Thus did not King Dauid, when he
said: I will keepe my strength to thee ô God,
that is, to serue thee. Offer not therefore to our Lord the dreggs of thy dotage, but the wine of thames ts, that is of
thy young and flourishing age.

Psal. 58.

Deut.32

Of sinners deferring to doe penance
S. Gregorie writeth thus: He doth not
shew himselfe to be a Christian by his
actions , that expecteth the time of
old age to doe penance , sithence he
hath no day of his life in his owne
power . Wherefore according to the
counsel of Isidorus: Euerie one ought
to hasten vnto God by penance, whiles
he may: least if he will not whiles he
                                    hath

hath power, he be in the end depriued
of so great a fauour. Delay not therefore (deare Christian brother) to doe
penance, least in the end thou be excluded with the foolish Virgins.

CHAPTER IIII.

Of flying and contemning the World.

LOue not the World (saieth S. Iohn in   I. Io. 2.
his canonical Epistle) nor those
things which are in the World. If any man
loue the World, the charitie of the Father is
not in him. Because all that is in the World,
is the concupiscence of the flesh, and the concupiscence of the eies, and the pride of life,
which is not of the Father, but is of the
world. And the World passeth, and the concupiscence thereof. S. Augustine trea-
ting vpon these wordes, saieth: What
is thy determination (ô man) either to
loue things temporal, and to passe
away with time: or to contemne the

world, and to liue with God for euer?
Doſt thou loue the world? it will ſwal-
low thee vp: it knoweth how to allure
men vnto it, but not how to afford
them any comfort. Truly the world is
like one that is excommunicated: for
that as our holy mother the Church
doth not pray for him that is excommunicated: ſo our Sauiour Ieſus Chriſt
prayed not for the world, who not-
withſtanding prayed for thoſe that
crucified him.

Io. 17.

Now what a foolish thing is it to
ſerue ſuch a maiſter or Lord, as is ac-
cuſtomed in the end to thruſt his ſer-
uaunt out of dores naked and without
any reward? And yet who ſeeth not
that this is the courſe or proceeding of
the world, towards thoſe that follow
it? Wherevpon we read of a certaine
Soldan of Babylon, who being grie-
uouſly ſick in the citie of Damaſcus,
and knowing that he could not liue
long, called for his ſtandard-bearer,
and ſaid vnto him: Thou art wont to
beare my banner to the warres, now
carrie the enſigne of my death (to wit
this little peece of cloath, that I am to

be

be shrouded in) throughout all Da-
mascus, saying: Behold the King of
the East dying, doth carrie nothing
with him, sauing onely this poore
peece of cloath. The like almost we
read of a certaine young King of Lor-
raine, who when he was at the point
of death, casting his eies to and fro
vpon the gorgeous buildings of his
pallace, brake forth into these wordes,
in the hearing of many of his subiects.
O good Iesu, how much is this world
to be contemned! Behold I that was
Lord of so many pallaces and places of
entertainement, know not whether I
must goe, or with whome I shall lodge
this night.

Forsake therefore (ô sinner) this thy
Sainct, to wit the world, before thou be
forsaken and left in so great pouertie
by it. Because as S. Iames affirmeth: *Ia. 4.*
Whosoeuer will be a friend of this World;
is made an enemie of God. And S. Gregorie auoucheth : By so much euerie one is nearer to God, by how
much he is estranged from the world.
For which cause our Sauiour would
suffer and be crucified without the ci-

tie, to the end he might shew, that he had no familiaritie with the world, and that whosoeuer doth desire to follow the fruit of his passion, must forsake the world, at least by affection and worldly conuersation. Wherevpon our Lord saieth by the Prophet Ieremie:

Iere.51. *Flie ye out of the middest of Babylon, and let euerie one saue his owne soule.* Babylon (according to S. Hierome) signifieth by interpretation the house of confusion, by which is ment the world; in which confusion now raigneth euerie where, aswell in the cleargie, as in the common people; aswell in the religious, as such as are secular; aswell in old men as in young: aswell in men, as in weomen: in so much that S. Iohn saieth verie well in his canonical Epistle: *The Whole World is set in Wickednes* .

1. Io. 5.

And therefore S. Bernard counselleth men to flie to Religion saying: Flie out of the middest of Babilon (that is out of the world to religion) flie I say, and saue your soules. Flie to the cities of refuge: where you may both doe penance for what is past, and obtaine

grace

grace in the prefent, and confidently
expect that glorie which is to come.
Let not the remorfe or remembrance
of your finnes hinder you, becaufe
where finne hath abounded, there
grace is wount to fuperabound : neither let the aufteritie of penance make
you affraid. For the paffions of this
time are not condigne to the former
fault which is remitted, nor to the prefent grace of comfort which is infu-
fed, nor to the future glorie which is
promifed vs, if we truly repent, and
contemne the world.

Howbeit fower reafons may be af-
figned, for which we ought to defpife
the world.

First wife men are wont to depart
from that place, which is infected
with the peftilence, or with any ill fauour or ftench : and especially when
they feele themfelues ill at eafe, or dif-
pofed to ficknes. The world is fuch a
contagious place, which containeth fo
many euills of finne and vice : for we
fee fo many ill fauoures and ftenches
of finne infecting our foules, which we
contract by our fenfes, as it were by
our

our nostrills. Wherefore sithence sinne is a contagious maladie : we ought to shunne the companie of the wicked ; because it is dangerous for such as are sound to dwell with those that are sick of a leaprie. For this cause Ecclesiasticus said : *He that toucheth* Eccl.13. *pitch shall be defiled With it: and he that cō̄municateth With the proud, shall put on pride.* S. Hierome also doth auouch the same. Nothing, saieth he, doth so much hurt men, as euill companie: according as a mās cōpanie is, such is he. A lambe and a woolfe cannot liue well together in one house : a chaste man flieth the companie of him that is luxurious: I thinke it a thing more then impossible, that a man can continue for any long time good, that vseth the company and conuersation of such as are lewd.

Not without iust cause therefore Psal.17. doth the Psalmist crie out: *With the holy thou shalt be holy and With the innocent man thou shalt be innocent : and With the elect thou shalt be elect ; and With the perverse thou shalt be peruerted.* But as bad companie or conuersation is verie hurtfull:

so good is exceeding profitable. Nothing can be compared to this treasure. He that findeth companie that is good and vertuous , findeth life , and floweth with riches : and to say the truth, a man seldome becōmeth good or bad , but by meanes of those, with whome he doth conuerse: for the heart of a young man is like vnto a table , whereon nothing is painted or written : whatsoeuer therefore he receiueth frō companie: that he keepeth (be it good or bad) vntill his dying day. Thus S. Hierome. Wherefore we ought to estrange our selues from the wicked world,by reason of the trouble of so bad a neighbour : for no neighbour can be so hurtfull, as the neighbourhood of sinners , of whome the world is full.

Secondly, wise men are wont to depart from those places , where they feare to be deliuered into the hands of their enemies : which kind of treacherie is committed in the world daily: for which cause it may well be thought to be like vnto the traytor Iudas , betraying his Lord and maister with a

Z   kisse,

Mat.26. kiſſe. Whomeſoeuer (ſaieth he) I ſhall kiſſe, *that is he, hold him*. Which wordes the world vſeth to the diuells : for whome the world kiſſeth in this preſent life, that is, exalteth to honoures and dignities, it deliuereth to his enemies, to wit, the diuells. Wherevpon S. Hierome ſaieth : It is a ſigne of manifeſt damnation, when a man obtaineth in the world whatſoeuer his heart deſireth, and is beloued of the world : he erreth in the way, who by riches and delightes haſtneth to goe to his countrie. Thus S. Hierome.

Thirdly wiſe men take heede of that place, where they feare any danger : howbeit the world is a place moſt dangerous, and full of ieopardie, and therefore in the holy ſcripture it is called a ſea. This made king Dauid to ſay: Pſa.103. *This great ſea, and verie large*. The danger of this ſea (ſaieth S. Bernard) is apparantly ſeene by the ſmall number of thoſe that paſſe ouer, and the multitudes that are drowned therein. It is like the Marſilian ſea, where ſcarce one of fower paſſeth ſecurely. In the ſea of this world, of fower ſoules ſcarce
one

one is faued. It is like the general deluge, where thofe that did efcape,
where verie few in refpect of thofe
that did perish. Finally it is like the
fierie fournace of Babylon, made hoat
by Nabuchodonofor, to wit the infernal Lucifer.

Wherefore euerie man ought to feare
the fame verie much, for that with the
winde of one onely worde he is enflamed with the fire of anger : with the
glance of a faire woman he is enflamed with the fire of vnchaft pleafure:
with the fight of any thig that is good,
he burneth with the flame of vnlawfull defire.

Fourthly we fee by experience, that a
wife man is varie, not to put himfelfe
into the companie of his mortal enemie. The diuel (being the prince of
this world) is our deadly enemie, and
feeketh our vtter ruine and calamitie,
from whome we flie, when we forfake
the world and all things tranfitorie.
Of whome the wife man biddeth vs
beware, when he faieth : *Be farre from
the man, that hath power to kill, and thou* Eccli. 9
shalt not fufpect the feare of death. This

Z 2   man

man is the diuel, who is called a man;
for that he was vanquished by a man.
Our Sauiour speaking of him, giueth
Mat.13. him this epitheton : *The enemie man*
(saieth he) *hath done this*; to wit, ouer-
sowen cockle among the wheate.

Wherefore we must note, that there
is no other meanes perfectly to subdue
the world, but to depart from it.
Wherevpon we read in the liues of the
Fathers, that S. Arsenius remaining as
yet in the Emperours pallace, desired
God, saying : Shew me, I beseech thee,
ô Lord, the way of saluation: And there
came a voyce, saying vnto him.
ARSENIVS FLIE MEN, AND THOV SHALT
BE SAVED : wherevpon he forthwith
departed from the court, and became
a Monke. At an other time he likewise
prayed to God, saying : Direct me,
ô Lord, in the way of saluation. And a
voyce said vnto him the second time:
ARSENIVS, FLIE, KEEPE SILENCE,
AND BE QVIET : FOR THESE ARE THE
ROOTES OF NOT SINNING For by flight
we ouercome the concupiscence of
the flesh, by silence the pride of life, by
quietnes, the concupiscéce of the eies,
or

or the desire of riches.

Also Isidorus exhorting vs to the cō-
tempt of the world, saieth: If thou desire to be quiet, couet nothing of the
world: cast from thee whatsoeuer may
hinder thy good purposes : be dead to
the world, and the world to thee: make
no more account of the glorie of the
world, then if thou were alreadie dead,
despise that whiles thou liuest, which
after death thou canst not possesse.

S. Hierome writing of this present
life, exclaimeth in this manner against
the vanitie and breuitie thereof. O
worldly life, not a life, but death; a deceitfull life, loaden with sorrowes : a
life that is weake, counterfait, and passing away like a shdow : now thou dost
flourish and blossome, and forthwith
thou dost fade away to nothing: being a
life depriuing vs of life, fraile, momē-
tanie, and fleeting. Who the more thou
dost encrease, the more thou dost de-
crease: the more thou goest fore   rd,
the more thou drawest towards a   a.
O life full of snares; how many m   in
the world dost thou intangl   w many for thy sake do alreadie feele the in-
                                    tole-

tolerable torments of hell? How happie is he, that perceiueth thy falshood and vncertainety? How much more happie, that careth not for thy faire wordes ād flatterie? But how most happie, that is well ridde of thee?

S. Augustine seeking to expresse how the world, flesh, and diuell vnite their forces in one, that they may preuaile against man, writeth thus of them. The world (saieth he) crieth, I will fade, the flesh crieth, I will kill: the diuel crieth, I will beguile: contrarily Christ sayeth, I will feede: and yet my proud mind will rather follow them that fade, then him that doth feede.

O deare Christian brother, if these things which thou hast now read, do not moue thee to the contempt of the world, listen yet to a more terrible speach of that blessed Father S. Bernard. Woe be to those (saieth he) for whome is prepared the anguish or gnawing of wormes, the scortching heate of fierie flames, continual thirst weeping, and gnashing of teeth, the dismall countenances of diuells. There death is desired, but not grāted: where there is no order, but euerlasti g horrour inhabiteth. How great griefe thinkest thou will there be then, how great sorrow, and lamentation, when the wicked shall be separated from the companie of the righteous, and be deliuered into the hands or power of the diuells, and shall goe with them into eternal torments: being neuer to be partakers of that vnspeakeable felicitie, but to be tormented in hell during all eternitie: where neither he that tormeteth, is at any time wearie; nor they that are tormented do at any time die: but they shall so die, that they may alwayes liue, and shall so liue, that they may always die.

Wherefore Isidorus saieth full well: If thou hadst the wisdome of Salomon, the strength of Sampson, the long life of Enoch: if thou hadst the power of Ptolomeus, the riches of Cræsus: what would all this profit thee, if thy flesh were giuen to the wormes, thy soule to the diuells, to be tormented with the rich glutton world without end?

Moreouer the shortnes of thy life, and vncertainty of thy death, ought to admo-

admonish thee to defpife this world,
and all things therein contained. Wherevpon S. Gregorie fayeth: the mindes
of reprobatemen, for that they thinke
that they shall remaine long in this
life, do doe many things amiffe: but
good men, for that they confider the
shortnes of their life, do shunne pride,
and the finnes of vncleannes.

Of the breuitie of this present life S.
Iames in the fourth chapter of his canonical Epistle writeth thus : *What is*
your life? It is a vapour appearing for a
little, and afterward it shall vanish away.
S. Augustine in effect faieth the same
thereof. The life of man, faieth he,
from his infancie to his dying day, is
but short, and foone paffeth away. If
Adam had liued vntill this verie prefent, and now were to giue vp the
ghoft, what good would his long life
doe him? And the fame holy father in
an other place faieth : Whatfoeuer
liueth for a time, doth shew by the
short fpace that it liueth, that this prefent life is nothing els, but a courfe or
voyage to death : in which no man is
permitted to stand still neuer fo little,

Iam. 4.

or

or to goe flowlie : but all are vrged foreward with like motion to make euerie day their dayes iourney towards the death of the bodie . Seneca a heathen Philofopher knew this full well, which caufed him to fay : We die euerie day : becaufe part of our life is daily taken away.

Behold deare Chriftiam brother , if thou confider thy felfe well, and ponder what I haue alreadie faid, and diligently marke with the eares of thy heart; what heereafter shall be mentioned: thou wilt plainely perceiue, that thou oughteft rather to fay , I trauaile towardes death: then to beleeue, that thou haft any long time to remaine heere vpon earth. Howbeit thou thinkeft that thou shalt liue yet many yeares, and poffeffe thy worldly goods,ioyes,and pleafures. But I feare thou wilt not find it fo : *For man* (as the Pfalmift faieth) *is made like vnto vanitie; his dayes paffe as a shadow.* Pfa. 143

Aa   CHAP.

CHAPTER V.

Of despising all transitorie riches, digni-
ties, and honourable offices.

Baruc. 3   VVHere are the Princes of the Gentiles, and they that rule ouer the
beasts, that are vpon the earth ? that play
with the birds of the heauen, that treasure
vp siluer, and gold, Wherein men haue confidence, and is there no end of their gettings
Which fashion siluer, and are carefull:
neither is there intention of their Workes:
They are destroyed, and are gone downe
to hell, and others are risen vp in their place.
Thus wrote the Prophet Baruch,
beholding the transitorie riches, dignities, and vanities of this world. Prosper
in his sentences prosecuteth the same
argumēt in this wise. Where are those,
to whome the chiefest citizens did sue
with cap and knee for promotion and
honours ? where are those excellent
Oratours ? where are those famous
con-

contriuers of fumptuous feafts and bã-
quets? Where are the braue breeders of
great horfes ? where are the Capi-
taines of armies? where are the Peeres
and Princes? Are they not all duft? are
not all ashes? Is not the hyftorie of
their life contained in a few verfes?
Looke vpõ the graues and fepulchers,
and tell me, who was the feruant, who
was the maifter, who was rich ? Difcerne, if thou canft, the prince from
the peafant, the ftróg from the weake,
the faire from the deformed . Thus
Profper in the place before mentioned.

Howbeit we muft note, that humane
glorie , from what thing foeuer it
doth proceed, is to be auoided. Firft, for
that it is moft moft vile according to
its effence. Secondly, for that it is moft
fickle and fraile in cõtinuance. Thirdly for that it is moft falfe in its promife
and performãce. Fourthly for that it
is moft perfidious in its recompence.
Firft therefore I fay that worldly glorie
is to be auoided and contemned by vs,
for that of its owne nature it is verie
bafe. Old Mathathias in the firft booke

of the Machabees affirmeth the same:
Be not affraid (saieth he) of the wordes of
of a sinnefull man : because is glorie is dung,
and worme:to day he is extolled,and to morrow he:hall not be found : because he is turned into his earth, and his cogitation is perished. What of all other things is more
base then dung? What among all liuing
creatures is more base thē a worme? If
therefore the vaine glorie of man is no
better then dung or a worme: men
haue iust reason rather to flie , then affect the same.

1.Mac. 2.

The glorie of the world is like vnto
rotten wood, which albeit it shine, and
make a faire shew in the night season:
yet it cannot be denied (as both philosophie teacheth , and experience
proueth) but that it is rotten. So man,
during the obscure night of this life,
ietteth vp and downe , and in the eies
of simple men seemeth to shine like a
second sunne : but this darknes being
departed, and death arriued, then it
appeareth what he is indeed : When our
Lord (Isay) shall come to iudgement , and
lighten the hidden things of darknes, and
manifest the counsells of mens hearts: then
those

1.Cor.4

those that seeme so glorious now in the eie of the world, will appeare to be much more vile and contemptible, the any rotten woode, and consequently not to be regarded or respected.

Such worldly gallants likewise are like vnto battes or reremise, who flie and flutter vp and downe in the dark, as if they were braue birdes indeed: but assoone as the day light approacheth, they hide themselues in holes, and appeare to be most ougly and deformed creatures; O if those men would consider these things, who glorie in their transitorie riches, and are puffed vp with pride, and contemne others by reflecting vpon their nobilitie, power, and dignitie, and the short felicitie of their stinking flesh, which albeit it be pampered neuer so much, must within a while returne into dust and ashes: if (I say) thy would seriously consider these things in their mind, ad withall how much more vile, loathsome, and deformed they are like to appeare (if they repent not) at the day of iudgement, I doubt not, but they would heartily detest the temporal glorie

glorie of this world: knowing this for
certaine, that it is impoſſible (as S. Hierome doth affirme) that any man appeare glorious both heere on earth,
and heereafter in heauen.

Secondly we ought to flie and auoid
the glorie of the world, for that it is
moſt fickle and fraile, and in no ſort
ſtable: for it is defectiue like a vapour,
or any other ſmokie ſubſtance, which
the more it is eleuated on high, the
more it is attenuated, vntill it wholy
vaniſh away: A flower, albeit it
smell neuer ſo sweet, and appeare neuer ſo faire for a time: yet it withereth,
and all the glorie thereof periſheth
with a little heate of the ſunne: like
vnto this, is the glorie of mortal men.
For ſo hath the Prophet Iſay affirmed:
All fleſh, ſaieth he, is graſſe, and all the glo-
rie thereof as the floWr of the field: the
graſſe Withereth, and the floWer falleth: and
the beautie of the shape thereof periſheth: So
the rich man (ſaieth S Iames) ſhall alſo
Wither in his Wayes.

The louers therefore of temporal
glorie and dignities are like to the
graſſe growing on the toppes of houſes,

Iſay. 40

Ia. 1.

Pſa. 128

                                    Which

Which is withered before it be plucked vp.
Wherevpon Ecclesiasticus saieth. *All* Eccl.10
power is of short life. In so much that he
which raigneth to day as a King or
Emperour, shall perchance to morrow
be carried to his sepulcher. For where
is now the glorie of King Assuerus, Either
who raigned fró India vnto Æthiopia 1.
ouer an hundred twentie seué prouin-
ces ? Where is now the glorie of Alexá- 1. Mac.
der the great, that made so many bat- 1.
tells, and obtained the munition of all,
and slew the kings of the earth, and
passed through out euen to the ends of
the world: and tooke the spoyles of the
multitude of the Gentiles: ád the earth
was silent in his sight ? What is now
become of all his greatnes and glorie?
Where are now so many thousands of
potentates and princes, that whilome
liued in this world in exceeding great
honour and dignitie ? Are they not all
sodainely passed away as pilgrimes or
guests, that remaine in a place but one
day onely: Verily it is so indeed: for not
one of them hath remained : Because
their dayes haue failed in vanitie, and their Psal.77.
        yeares

yeares in haſt. Heerevpon a certaine
old poet ſaid verie well.

> God *hath decreed that all liue ſubiect*
>   *vnto death,*
> And *do ſurrender vp to him their vitall*
>   *breath.*
> Death *With his fatal ſithe all liuing things*
>   *cutts downe:*
> He'es *partial vnto none: ſpares neither*
>   *King nor cloWne.*

Thirdly we ought to flie and auoid
the glorie of this world, for that it is
moſt falſe, and keepeth promiſe with
none. For what Emperour, or princely
potentate hath it not deceiued? Becauſe it promiſeth a long and honourable life to its followers, together with
much power and peace, whereas it is
vnable to adde ſo much as one momēt
of time to the length of their liues.
Who was euer like to Alexander the
great in temporal glorie? who neuer
loſt any battell, but contrariwiſe with
a few ſouldiers oftimes ouerthrew
whole armies. He neuer beſieged any
citie, which he did not winne; nor in-
uaded any countrie, which he brought
not into ſubiection: and yet notwith-
                              ſtanding

standing when he thought that all the world had beene his owne, and that no man from thence foreward would haue resisted him; then he was poysoned, and died on a sodaine.

Why thē are men so madde a sto hunt after the glorie of the world, which can stand them in no steede at the hower of their death, when ordinarily they are in greatest neede ? Wherevpon Petrus Blesensis in a certaine epistle writeth thus : The glorie of the world being false and deceitfull, deludeth those that loue the same : for whatsoeuer it pretendeth for the present, or promiseth for the time to come, all shall come to nothing, as water running downe. Psal. 57.

Fourthly the glorie of the world is worthily to be contemned and auoided by vs, for that it is most perfidious in its recompence: because it doth not guide a man to glorie and celestial happines, but to shame and perpetual torments. Wherevpon almightie God saieth by the mouth of the Prophet Osee: *Their glorie I will change into igno-* Osee.4. *minie.* Yea he will change their power

Bb   into

into weakenes, their wifdome into foolishnes, and all their pleafure and mirth into exceffiue forrow and anguish. For according to the meafure of their finne, fuch shall be the meafure of their paine.

S. Hierome fpeaking vnto the louers of temporal glorie, thundreth out this terrible Væ againft them : Woe be to you (faieth he) who haften towards the kingdome of heauen in the way of riches: feing *it is eafier for a camel to paffe* **Mat.19** *through the eie of a needle, then for a rich* **Marc.** *man to enter into the kingdome of heauen.* **10.** Thefe are not my wordes,but the wor-**Luc.18.** des of Chrift. If thefe wordes may be reuoked, Chrift is not God : for he faieth in an other place : Heauen and **Mat.24.** earth shall paffe, but my wordes shall not paffe.

Howle ô you wretched worldlings, proud, and puffed vp with the wind of vnconftāt fortune: who defpife others, and tread them vnder foote (for that forfooth they are not gentlemen borne) being blinded with worldly vanities, and the fmoke of false honours, dignities and promotion: when as notwithstanding the webbe of your short life will peraduenture be cut off by death this verie night, as the webbe is wont to be cut off by the weauer, and you throwne downe into hell, there to be most cruelly tormented for euer: continually dying, yet alwayes liuing: liuing I say in euerlasting torments, which shall torment you more then other men : for sithence in your life you liue not in labour like other men: yea not onely refuse to labour for the gaining of heauen, but also hinder others that would labour and vse vio- lence for the obtaining of the same; for this reason you shalbe scourged with the diuells, and not with men: For the more you abound in this world in glorie, riches, and pleasure, the more paine (assure your selues) will be infli- cted vpon you heereafter.

Psal. 72.

But what neede I vse so many wor- des, since we want not examples ? Christ comming into the world chose twelue Apostles, whereof one onely (to wit. S. Bartholomew) was by birth a gentle man: and one onely (to wit S. Matthew, and this before he was ele-

&ed to be an Apoſtle) was a follower
and friend of worldly riches and promotion : all the reſt were poore fisher
men. Now ſithence it is ſo, and Chriſt
is the truth it ſelfe, and whatſoeuer he
ſaieth cannot be falſe : it followeth
that there are verie few gentlemen fit
for heauen : for that inordinately
louing themſelues, ād worldly riches,
honoures, and pleaſures, they walke
the direct way that leadeth downe to
hell, and will infallibly find themſelues there eare they are aware, vnleſſe they repent, and begin to doe
well.

But perchance one that is blinded
with ignorance, will wonder at this,
and aske me, how this can be? To
whome I replie : Do we not firmely
beleeue, that a man for one mortal
ſinne (if he die vnrepentant) ſhall be
damned? If this be ſo (he will ſay) then
doubtleſſe ſcarce one of tenne thouſand will be ſaued, eſpecially of rich
men, and ſuch as liue amidſt the pleaſures and contentments of the world.
For what els commonly (eſpecially in
theſe our dayes)is a gentle má,but as it
were

were a bladder blowne full of the wind
of vaine glorie and earthly reputation, or as it were a vessell replenished with the stinking dreggs of all
sortes of sinnes? For where shall you
finde luxurie, couetousnes, and pride
so frequent as amongst the rich, noble,
and mightie men of the world?

Moreouer are they not theeues and
robbers, who violently defraud poore
men of their hire? Who oppresse and
kill those, whome they ought to relee-
ue and nourish with the goods which
God hath giuen them for the mainte-
nance of the poore? They superabound
in apparell and costly fare, and care not
if the poore in the interi starue through
cold and hunger. They erect great pallaces and stately houses, that they may
be admired by mortal eies, suffering
the poore to lie crying in the stree tes,
oppressed with many maladies and
miseries. They often make feastes for
such as are rich, and stuffe their pan-
ches full of delicate fare, permitting
their poore brethren to starue for hunger. Neither do they stay heere, but
proceede fur ther, passing from one ini-

quitie

quitie to an other. For after gluttonie
followeth leacherie. I am ashamed to
say any more. And indeede I am vnable
to recount the least part of the enormious crimes which thy commit. The
tonges of all mortall men would first
faile, before they would be able to expresse them all. In so much that by
their carriage they seeme neither to acknowledge, that there is a God, that
seeth all their actions; or that after
death they shall render an accompt of
their doings.

Howbeit that man easily falleth into sinne, that considereth not the mortalitie of his being, and that God is to
be his iudge at the day of doome. Verily he is ignorant and foolish, that is
vnmindfull of these things, and doth
not despise these worldly allurements,
and diuellish enticements. And to say
the truth, if they did acknowledge God
to be their iudge, and would giue credit to those that know these things to
be so, better then themselues, I thinke
they would not sinne with so little re-
morse of conscience.

Moreouer when these wretched
world-

worldlings goe to the Church, is it (thinke you) deuoutly to heare maße, or tó frequent the ſacraments? Surely no: but rathet to contẽmplate the faire faces of the prettie wenches, that are preſet. Theſe are the bookes, in which they read, this is the knowledge, which they haue of God. The thoughts and meditations of their minds are likewiſe buſied about diuerſe voyages which they pretend both by ſea and land, and how they may encreaſe their riches, and aduance their owne, and their childrens fortune.

In their apparell they are exceeding coſtly and curious: addiᶜted to playing, tilting, dancing, courting, and drinking, and ſuch like vices: they alternatim make great banquets one for an other: intermingling wine ãd weomen together: that ſo (if it were poſſible) they might glut themſelues with pleaſure, and ſatiat their vnſatiable deſire. But alas (ó you wicked and wretched worldlings) what do you meane? Do you not know that by ſo doing, you deſtroy both bodie and ſoule before the time? For whence
ensue

enfue fo many ficknesses and vntimely
deathes to fo many men, but from o-
uermuch eating and drinking, and im-
moderate vfe of woemen? You thinke
that you do deceiue God: but certainely you deceiue your felues. You fat-
té your bodies, but forget your foules:
and by fo doing, deftroy them both before the time.

But fithence it is impoffible to per-
fuade you to doe otherwife; reioyce,
and make merrie during this short
fpace of time that remaineth, as much
as you will, that afterwards you may
lamét for euer with the diuells in hell.
If you like this courfe, loofe no time:
get you as many fuites of apparell as
you can, leaft you be contemned as if
you were clownes, and not gentlemen: fuffer no man to furpaffe you, or
put you downe, and fo you shall be
fure to be replenished in hell with
shame and confufion. What will then
become of your banquets, and dilicate
dishes? What will then become of your
pretious wines, mixt with aromatical
fpices? What will then become of your
daintie fare and drunkenes? For after
　　　　　　　　　　　　　death

death all these things will cease: after death I say there will be no more
quaffing, but you shall wish, being
in hell, with that rich glutton (*Who*   Luc.16.
was cloathed with purple and silke,
and fared delitiously euerie day) for a drop
of cold water to coole your tongue,
and shall not obtaine the same. Sow in   Galat.6.
corruption, and you shall reape corruption at the day of dome: when Christ
the eternal king shall say vnto you
together with the rest of the repro-
bate standing at his left hand: *Get you*   Mat.25.
away from me you accursed into fire euer-
lasting, which was prepared for the diuell,
and his angells.

Woe be to thee ô hard hearted sinner, if thou repent not before that terrible and dreadfull day: in which thou
must render an accompt, not onely of
thy lasciuiousnes, excesse in apparell,
drunkennes, gluttonie, and the time   Mat.12.
which thou hast lost or spent in vaine,
but also of euerie idle worde, which
thou hast spoken. Why ô wretch dost
thou not amend, why dost thou delay
from day to day to turne to our Lord?
Why dost thou not presently repent,

C c   and

and be sorrowfull for thy sinnes? Behold death maketh haste, and commeth running after thee day and night, hoping to take thee vnawares, and so to trip vp thy heeles. The diuel likewise maketh haste, to the end that assoone as death hath surprized thee, he may seize vpon thee, and hale thee downe headlong with him into eternal torments and miserie. Thy riches (of whome thou dost now so much vaunt and glorie) will then forsake thee in thy greatest necessitie. Finally the wormes expect thy bodie, which now thou dost nowrish so carefully, to the end they may gnaw and deuoure it, and so let it lie rotten vntill the day of iudgement: at which time being revnited to the soule, it may togither with the same receiue infinit torments in hell.

Why dost thou wander to and fro amidst the craggie path-wayes of the vanities of this world, seaking content in riches, honoures, and dignities, where it is not to be found? Heere thou wilt find no true pleasure, for that there is none heere. But if thou desire

true

true comfort and confolation, haften towardes the happines of that heauenly Hierufalem : there certainely are the true ioyes, *Which neither eie hath* ſeene, *nor eare hath heard, neither haue they aſcended into the heart of man.* Forſake therefore (I beſeech thee) theſe things that are temporal, and ſubiect to corruption ; that thou maieſt attaine to thoſe that are eternal and euerlaſting.

1. Cor. 2

But alas what ſhall I ſay to thoſe men, who neither for the loue of God, nor for feare of his indignation, nor for dread of death, nor for terrour of torments, nor for horrour of hell and eternal damnation, abſtaine from ſinne? but are ſorrowfull that they cannot liue heere for euer : that ſo (if it were poſſible) they might ſatiate their vnſatiable deſire with wicked worldly pleaſure ? Woe be to you that laugh heere, for you ſhall lament heereafter. Woe be to you, that wiſh for theſe temporal ioyes and contentments: becauſe they ſhall be taken from you, euen againſt your wills ; and in lieu of them you ſhall haue helliſh torments.

Behold you haue yet a little time left:

Cc 2   during

during this, accomplish the measure of your miseries or malice, to the end, that Gods whole wrath may rush vpon you at the day of reuenge. Enioy (during this short time) your sports and recreation : giue your selues asmuch as you will, to quaffing, quarrelling, dauncing, and courting : Your time is but short, and therefore be not idle : during those few dayes or yeares of your life, which are yet behind, be merrie and Iouial ; for that after death (vnlesse you améd in the meane while) you must resolue to lament for euer with the diuells in hell. Heape riches together for your children, enlarge your territories, rack your tenants, amplifie your power, augment your nobilitie and fame ; that your children (when yon are dead and gone) may ratifie the euill deedes which you haue done in your life time, to the end you may endure the greater torments with them in the prison of euerlasting perdition.

But some man will answere, saying: God is mercifull, and full of compassion : who receiueth and forgiueth
eue-

euerie sinner, that returneth vnto him.

All this I graunt to be true, and that God is more mercifull, then man's heart can imagin, and pardoneth euerie one, that at time fitting returneth vnto him. Is he not most merciful (thinke you) and full of patience, who endureth so many iuiuries at the hands of sinners, and giueth thē time and space to repent and doe penance? But yet know this, that as he is most mild in suffering, so he is most seuere in punishing.

Some man will obiect againe. That he that in his whole life did neuer any good action, if he repent at the hower of death, and doe penance for his offences, shall obtaine pardon and forgiuenes. O how vaine is this imagination, how foolish is this cogitation. Certainely I thinke that of a hundred thousand that put off their conuersion vntill their last end, scarce one of them is saued. For he that hath beene borne and trayned vp in sinne from his verie childehoode, how cā such a one know how to demaund pardon and grace of God?

God? who hath neither liued according to God, nor knowne him: nor
could euer endure to heare of him:
who acknowledgeth not his sinne, nor
euer knew what penance did meane,
vnlesse perchance in a dreame: being
likewise as yet wholy entangled with
the businesses and affaires of the world
whome the care of his childrē (whome
he must forsake) oppresseth; whome
infirmitie of bodie disquiteth: whome
the griefe of his riches and temporal goods tormēteth; for that he seeth,
that he cannot now enioy them any
longer. How small (may we imagin)
is such a mans repentance , who, if he
were not sick, or hoped not for reco-
uerie, would not aske forgiuenes?

Wherefore for a conclusion I auouch,
that he , that feareth not to offend God
whiles he is young and in health , will
hardly obtaine mercie of God at the
hower of his death. For who can imagin that repentāce to be good ād syn-
cere, which a man maketh, for that he
perceiueth , that he can liue no longer?
Who if he should recouer , would liue
much worse thē before. I haue knowne
                                        some

some (saieth S. Hierome,) who hauing
beene dangerously sick , and in their
sicknes hauing done penance; haue afterwards growne well in bodie, but in
soule farre worse. This is mine opinió,
this I hold to be true , and by often experience haue found it to be so, that his
end is seldome or neuer good , whose
life hath beene alwayes lewd : who
hath not feared to offend, but hath có-
tinually liued amidst the pleasures or
commodities of the world. Thus S.
Hierome.

Wherefore deare Christian brother,
if thou be wise, if thou haue eies to see
the danger of worldlings , despise and
forsake all these things; to wit, the false
glorie of the world , and transitorie
riches , for his sake that is aboue all
things. For *What doth it profit a man, if he* Mat.16.
gaine the World , and sustaine the damage of Marc.8.
his soule? Know that thou art a man, and Luc.9.
that worldly glorie is a hinderance of
grace: yea (which is worse) the deadly
enemie of eternal happines : for what
man do we read, to haue euer passed
from worldly delightes to perpetual
pleasures ?

O

O how deceitfull and vaine is the glorie that men feeke and receiue one from an other, and the glorie which is of God onely, they feeke not! That man, which defireth to be preferred before others, is he not a fit companion for him, that faid: I *Will afcend into hea-* *uen, aboue the ftarres of God I Will exalt my* *throne, I Will fit in the mount of the tefta-* *ment, in the fides of the north. I Will* *afcend aboue the height of the cloudes,* *I Will be like to the higheft* ? Howbeit let him feare, leaft mounting vp with Lucifer into a chaire of eftate, he tumble not downe headlong, and breake his owne necke.

Ifai. 14

O how happie and bleffed is he, who placeth his whole affection in the defire of eternitie : who is neither extolled with profperitie, nor deiected with aduerfitie : and fo hauing nothing in the world, which he affecteth, there is nothing in the world, which he feareth. And in verie deede the glorie of this world is nothing els, but as it were a puff of winde, paffing by our eares. How wonderfully art thou blinded then (deare Chriftian brother) and how

fen-

senseles dost thou shew thy selfe to be,
if thou seeke after worldly glorie. For
as S. Anselme doth affirme: Thou canst
not be in honour without labour and
paine, nor in prelacie or office without
affliction, nor in dignitie without vanitie of minde. Wherefore if thou
wouldest prudently consider the danger which thou dost incurre by coue-
ting the honours, riches, and dignities
of the world, thou wouldest doubtlesse
abstaine from them, as the hurts and
hinderances of thy chiefest good.

CHAPTER VI.

*Of the continual feare and expectation,
which we ought to haue of death.*

REmember (saieth the wise man) *that* Eccli.14
death slacketh not. Many are the benefits which arise vnto vs by the frequent meditation and remembrance
of death, which is declared in diuerse
places of holy scripture. One place

D d   shall

shall serue for all, taken out of Eccle-
Eccli.7. siasticus: *Remember*, saieth he, *thy later
ends , and thou wilt not sinne for euer.*
By our later ends he meaneth death,
iudgement, hell, and heauen. This caused S. Bernard to say : Man's chiefe
Philosophie, is to meditate of death
continually: this meditation, whither-
soeuer he goeth, let him carrie with
him in his memorie , and he will not
sinne eternally. S. Augustine likewise
saieth : Nothing doth so much recal a
man from sinne, as the frequent meditation of death. For it is this, that maketh a man to humble himselfe , to
contemne all things; and to doe , or
willingly accept of penance. And S.
Hierome : He easily contemneth all,
that continually considereth himselfe
to be mortal.

Firſt he contemneth the concupiscence of the eies, when he considereth,
that he muſt so sodainely forsake all
things: secondly the concupiscence of
the flesh , when he calleth to remembrance, that his bodie shall shortly be
meate for wormes : thirdly the pride
of life, when he entreth into consideration,

tion, that he that will now be exalted
aboue other men, shall within a while
be laid vnder ground, and be troden
vpon by the feete of euerie one.

O that the kings and mightie Princes
of the world would confider, after
what manner they are to be carried
from their ftately pallaces to a ftrict
and narow fepulcher : from their pallaces fo delightfull and cleare, to their
fepulcher fo dreadfull and obfcure:
frō their pallaces painted with flowers,
ād adorned with images, to their fepulchers full of ill fauoures and ftenches:
from their pallaces fo full of plentie, to
their fupulchers fo poore and emptie:
finally from their pallaces replenished
with children and feruants, to their
fepulchers depriued of all thefe
things.

O where is their former pompe?
where is their glorie paft ? where are
now the troupes of their attendants?
where are now their gay and glittering
garments ? and all their other ornaments? Loe he that a little before liued
in his pallace, paffing his time in delights and pleafure, is now eaten by
Dd 2   wormes

wormes, lying in his sepulcher. Alas deare brethren, (saieth Pope Innonocentius) consider, how he that a little before sate in his house rich and renowned, lieth now poore in his tôbe: how he that walked in his court glorious and respected, lieth now in his graue, deformed and contemned: how he that was fed with the rarest fare in his priuie chamber, is now consumed with wormes in his sepulcher.

Of the profitable remembrance of death S. Peter Damian, a Monke of the holy Order of S. Bennet, and Cardinal of Ostia, writing to a certaine Countesse, sayeth thus: It is good, often to call to remembrance, how the time being now come, in which the sinnefull soule beginneth to be separated from the bandes of the flesh, with how grieuous feare shee is terrified, with how great anguish of an afflicted conscience shee is tormented. Shee remembreth the things forbidde, which shee hath committed: shee beholdeth the commandements of God, which through negligence and côtempt shee hath omitted. Shee grieueth, that the time,

time, which shee had to doe penance, hath beene so vainely employed: shee groneth, that the immutable moment of seuere reueng is so neere at hand, not possibly to be auoided. Shee would faine stay; shee is forced to depart. Shee would faine recouer what shee hath lost, and cannot be heard. Shee looketh backward vpon the course of her whole life past, and esteemeth it to be but as it were one onely pace: shee looketh forward, and seeth infinite worlds of time, which shall neuer haue end. Shee lamenteth therefore, for hauing lost the ioyes of all eternitie, which shee might haue gained so quickly. Shee weepeth likewise, that for so short pleasure of the alluring flesh, shee is bereaued of the vnspeakeable sweetnes of euerlasting happines. Shee blusheth to see, that for that substance sake, which is to be meate for wormes, shee hath neglected that, which should haue beene placed among the quires of Angells.

At length shee lifteth vp the eies of her minde, and considering the glorie of the inmortal riches of heauen, shee

is

is ashamed, that for the loue of the beggerie of his present life, shee hath lost that glorie. Againe when shee looketh downeward vpon the vale of this world, as vpon a mist, and contrariwise seeing aboue her the brightnes of that eternal light, shee plainely perceiueth, that that which shee loued, was but darknes and night.

O if shee could obtaine the fauour to haue some little time allotted to doe penance and satisfaction, how austere would shee be in her life and conuersation? How many and how great matters would shee promise to performe? How strictly would shee binde her selfe to pietie and deuotion?

In the meane season, whiles the eie-sight faileth; whiles the heart panteth, whiles the throat (the voyce being lost) doth draw breath with difficultie, whiles the teeth by little and little grow black, and as it were rustie: whiles the contenance groweth pale, and all the members of the bodie become stiffe through colde; whiles these things (I say) and other such like happen

pen

pen, as certaine signes of death approaching, all her workes and wordes present themselues before her, yea her verie thoughts are not wanting, and all these giue bitter testimonie against her, as against their author. All her sinnes and iniquities are layed as it were in heapes before her eies, and these which shee is vnwilling to see, shee is forced to behold, whether shee will or no.

Moreouer on the one side of her, shee beholdeth a terrible troup of dreadfull diuells; on the other side a multitude of heauenly Angells. The soule, that lieth in the midest, quickly perceiueth, to which of these two companies shee appertaineth. For if there be seene in her the signes and tokens of goodnes, shee is comforted by the comfortable speeches of the Angells; and by the sweetnes of their harmonious melodie, shee is allured to issue forth of the bodie. Contrariwise, if the darknes of her deserts, and the deformitie of her filthines do adiudge her to the left hand, shee is forthwith stroken with intolerable feare, shee is
trou-

troubled through the force of the sodaine violence , that is vsed : shee is throwne downe headlong and aſſaulted, and (poore ſoule) is forcibly plucked out of the priſon of the fleſh, that shee may be drawne to eternal torments with vnſpeakeable bitternes. This liuely deſcription maketh this holy Father Peter Damian of the dolefull eſtate of a ſinnefull ſoule at the hower of death.

The ſoule being thus ſeparated frō the bodie , looketh round about her hither and thither in hope of ſuccour, ād finding none, becometh exceeding ſorrowfull and ſad , if shee be to be dāned ; and breaketh forth into this lamentable exclamation: O thou accurſed ſoule! the ſoule rather of a mōſter, then of a man : the ſoule of a theefe, robber , adulterer, and excommunicated perſon : the ſoule of a fornicatour, vſurer , and of one forſworne : now thou ſeeſt)though too too late) the effects and fruits of ſinne.

Whiles the vnhappie ſoule looketh thus round about her ſpeaking to her ſelfe is this or the like manner, shee eſ-
pieth

pieth her garment, which in Baptisme
shee receiued white and free from all
spot and bleamish, become now more
black then either crow or pitch. This
dolefull sight causeth her to fetch a
most deepe sigh, and with bitter teares
and weeping, to make this lamentation. Alas, alas, who hath changed my
garment? Was not my garment heeretofore whiter then any snow? But
now (alas) I see it more filthy then
pitch, more black then any crow. Then
the diuel, that was wont to seduce her
vnto sinne, and whose pestiferous per-
swasions shee followed, whiles shee
liued in the world, appeareth vnto her
saying: My deare soule, wonder not:
it is I that haue prepared for thee this
garment: but thou alone art not thus
cloathed, but the greater part of the
whole world. Then the soule asketh:
who art thou? The diuel answereth:
Did I not euen now tell thee, that it is
I, that haue prepared this garment for
thee; Moreouer, I haue shewed thee
my life and couersation, and thou (like
a good soule) hath beleeued me,
and obeyed me in all things: thou hast

Ee

laboured with me, and put in execution whatsoeuer I haue willed thee : and therefore thou shalt dwell with me in a kingdome, which was prepared for me not for thee: where there is mourning without mirth, hunger without meate, where there is thirst without drink, darknes without light : where there is stech without any thing that is sweete, anguish without any comfort: where there is wayling without mitigation, weeping without intermission: where there is crying without silence, howling without sweetnes: where there is an vnquenchable fire without cooling, a boysterous winde without calme: where there is cold without any meane heate without any end, and all manner of euill without any good. O my darling, arise, and come with me: behold the angells of hell come to meete thee, and will sing vnto thee a song of sorrow and sadnes, a canticle full of bitternes and anguish.

Thē the Angell of God, who by God's appointment had the charge of her, shall likewise appeare vnto her, saying in this sort : Blessed are they, who liuing

liuing in the world, do take heede of
this moſt filthy garment. O how vnhappie art thou, ò darling of the diuell,
ò accurſed creature, who art ſo odious
in the ſight of thy Creator. I haue
beene with thee, and thou haſt not
ſeene me: I haue taught thee, and thou
wouldeſt not vnderſtand me : I haue
aduized thee, and thou wouldeſt not
heare me : wherefore depart into the
handes of the diuells : depart (I ſay)
into that place of torments, vnto
which thou art worthily adiudged according to thy workes.

But now (alas) what mortal man is
able to conceiue, much leſſe to expreſſe, in what deſpitefull manner the
furious fiends do aſſault this vnhappie
ſoule, and inſulting ouer her with
many ſcoffs and tants, do with their
fierie forkes and hellish inſtruments,
hale her downe headlong into euerlaſting torments. In the way they vpbraid her of her ſinnes, ſaying vnto her
in ſcoffing manner: O how braue haſt
thou beene heeretofore? how daintily
haſt thou beene fed? how gallantly
apparailed? how ſtrong and valiant

haft thou beene, and how fortunate?
Tell vs: where is now thy good cheere?
where is now thy braue attire ? why
doft thou not cark and care to fcrape
vp riches ? why doft thou not recreat
thy felfe with thy wife and children,
and with thy friends and acquaintance ? Why doft thou not fpeake to
them ?

Then the wretched foule shall begin
to curfe her bodie, faying: O temple
of the diuel : thy workes haue defiled
me: ô accurfed carcaffe, ô habitation of
fatan: arife quickly and come with me;
that thou maieft fee the torments,
which are prepared for me for thy fake:
in which I am to remaine vntill the
day of doome, and afterwards thou
shalt be with me for euer in the fame
damnation. Accurfed be thy eies,
which would not fee the light of truth,
and the way of God's iuftice. Accurfed
be thine eares, which would not heare
the wordes of eternal happines. Accurfed be thy noftrills , which would not
admit the fweete fauour of facred vertues. Accurfed be thy lipps and tongue,
which haue not tafted the fweete de-
                                    lights

lights of that eternal countrie, nor beene employed in the praise of God almightie. Accursed be thy handes, for that by them workes of charitie haue not beene practised towards the poore and needie. Accursed be thy verie heart and bowells, which haue belched vp such wicked counsell. Accursed be thy feete, which haue not frequented the churches of Christ. Accursed be thy members, ô thou accursed carion: for that they haue not desired the ioyes of heauen. Accursed be all thine actions, for that they haue iustly merited eternal torments.

Behold most (deare Christian brother) the surpassing great danger and feare, which are like to befall thee at thy last hower: from which notwithstanding thou maiest easily free thy selfe, if now thou be alwayes fearefull, and suspitious of death. Endeauour now to liue in that vertuous manner, as that at the hower of thy departure, thou mayest rather reioyce, then feare. Learne now to die to the world, that then thou mayest begin to liue with Christ thy Lord. Learne now to contemne

temne all things transitorie, that then
thou mayest be able to goe speedily
with Christ to eternal glorie. Now cha-
stise thy bodie by penance, that then
thou mayest haue an assured confidence.

O how happie and prudent is that
man, who endeauoureth to be such in
his life, as he would wish to be found
at the hower of his death. Wherefore I
aduise thee, to doe now whatsoeuer
lieth in thy power, for that thou knowest not the time of thy departure, nor
what will happen vnto thee after that
dreadfull hower. Do not relie vpon
thy friends and acquaintance, because
they will forget thee sooner then thou
dost imagin. If thou be not carefull for
thy selfe now whiles thou art liuing,
who will take care for thee when thou
art dead and gone? It is better to prouide now in time, and to send some-
thing that is good before hand, then
to relie vpon the assistance of other
men. Whiles thou hast time gather together immortal riches by giuing of
almes: now procure the Sainds of God
by thy deuout prayers to be thy friends:
that

that so, for thy vertuous actions they may receiue thee into those eternal tabernacles.

S. Gregorie giueth vs the same counsel, saying : We ought to haue a care, and daily to consider with great weeping, what a strict reckoning we must render vnto almightie God of all our actions, at the day of his comming. S. Bernard likewise maketh this soliloquie or secret speech vnto his soule. What a feare (saieth he) will that be ô my soule: when thou alone (all those things being forsaken, whose presence and sight are now so delightfull and pleasing) shalt enter into that vnknowne region, and shalt see those ougly horned monsters comming in troupes to meete thee, and readie to rush vpon thee? Who will occurre to helpe thee on the day of so great necessitie? Who will defend thee from those roaring lions, readie to deuour thee? who will comfort thee? who will conduct thee?

Howbeit the holy Angells will come and meete the soules of the righteous, driuing away the diuells, that they
hinder

hinder not their paſſage, and condu-
cting them with ioy to eternal happines. As for the ſoules of the wicked S.
Bernard ſaieth in an other place, that
they are affrighted at their departure
out of the bodie, aſhamed as they paſſe
in the way, and confounded at the
ſight of God's glorie. Wherevpon ex-
pounding that verſe of the 33. Pſalme,
Mors peccatorum peſsima. The death of ſin-
Pſal.33. ners is verie ill: He vſeth theſe wordes:
Their death is ill, in the loſſe of the
world, becauſe they cannot without
griefe be ſeparated from that which
they loued. It is worſe in the diſſolutiō
of the fleſh, for that their ſoules are
pulled out of their bodie by the diuells.
It is verie ill, or worſt of all in the torments of hell, when both ſoule end bodie ſhall be adiudged together to perpetual fire.

Wherefore conſider often, deare
brother, that death cannot be auoided: that the hower of death cannot be
knowne before hand: that the time
preordained of God cannot be changed: onely a good life cauſeth it to be
deſired, and willingly embraced. Verily

ly (saieth S. Bernard in the place before mentioned) the death of a iust
man is good in respect of rest and trá-
quillitie: better in respect of noueltie:
best of all by reason of securitie.

※※※※※※※※※※※※※※※※※※※※

CHAPTER VII.

*Of the ioyes of heauen, and paines
of hell.*

NEither eie hath seene, nor eare hath
heard, neither hath it ascended into
the heart of man, What things God hath
prepared for them, that loue him . Thus
wrote S. Paul of the glorie of heauen,
who albeit he had beene a eiewitnes of
the same, foūd it to surpasse all humane
vnderstanding and explication. O sin-
full soule, consider attentiuely the
greatnes and immmensitie of the heauenly glorie, that so all things transitorie may seeme base and contemptible vnto thee. Verily the ioyes of heauen are so great, and so many, that all

1. Cor.
2.

F f   the

the Arithmiticians in the world are
not able to count them: all the Geome-
tricians are not able to meafure them,
all the Gramarians, Logitians, and
Rhetoricians are not able to explicate
or expreffe them : becaufe neither eie
hath feene, nor eare hath heard, neither
hath is afcended into the heart of man,
what things God hath prepared for
them, that loue him. For all the Sainɛts
fhall reioyce at the fight of God aboue
them: at the beautie of the heauens ād
other fpiritual creatures beneath thē,
at the glorie of their bodie within
them, at the company of the holy
Angels and Sainɛts neere or about
them.

S. Anfelme reckoneth vp feuen
guifts or dowries, which the bodies of
the righteous shall haue in heauen: and
thefe are beautie, agilitie, ftrength,
libertie, health, pleafure, and long
life.

First therefore he affirmeth, that in
that happie life, the beautie of the iuft
shall be equall to the beautie of the
funne, which then shall be feuen times
brighter then it is now. Wherevpon it

is

is written : *The iust shall shine like the* Mat.13. *sunne, in the sight of* God.

Secondly their agilitie (which is a thing no lesse pleasing then beautie) shall be so great, as that they shall be as nimble as the verie Angells of God, who passe from heauen to the earth, and from the earth to heauen, sooner then cá be imagined. Of this agilitie or swiftnes we may likewise see an example in a beame of the sunne, which immediatly assoone as the sunne is risen in the East reacheth vnto the farthest parts of the West, that thereby we may see that that is not impossible, which we say of our future agilitie: especiallie sithence things liuing are wont to be more nimble, then such as are void of life.

Thirdly they that shall merit to be of the happie companie of those heauenly citizens, shall haue so great strength and force, that nothing shall be able to withstand them, (if they desire either to moue it, or push it out of its place) but it shall presently yeeld or giue way vnto them. Neither shall they find greater difficultie, in that

F f 2   which

which I say ; then we do now in the mouing of our eie. Let not (I pray you) that similitude of the Angells depart from our mind, which we shall haue in the world to come : to the end, that if in this, or in any thing els which we shall say heereafter, some other example do not occurre to our remembrance : let this suffice, that in that celestial happines we shall be like to the Angells.

Fourthly therefore sithence we shall be like vnto them, we shall likewise attaine to the like libertie or freedome. Wherefore like as nothing doth withstand the Angells, neither can any thing hinder or restraine them, but that they can most freely penetrate all things at their pleasure : so there shall be no obstacle, that may hinder vs : no enclosure that may in any sorte resist vs : no element, that shall neuer so little diobey our desire.

Fifthly in the life to come, man shall be so sound, that he shall in no sort be sick, but shall enioy surpassing great health. Of this health what can better be said, then what the Psalmist doth sing:

sing : *The health* (saieth he) *of the iust is* Psa.136.
of our Lord. To whome then true health
shall be giué of our Lord, what sicknes
shall be able to take it away? Verily we
may well beleeue, and (as I thinke)
vndoubtedly affirme, that the health
of the life to come, shalbe so continual,
immutable, and inuiolable ; that it
shall fill a man wholy with a certaine
vnspeakeable sweetnes of suauitie:
and driue away and put to flight, what
in it selfe may pretend the suspition of
any alteration, change, or hurt.

Sixthly in that future life, a certaine
pleasure or delight, that cannot be
vttered, shall inebriat the good, and,
through an inestimable sweetnes,
which it containeth in it selfe, shall sa-
ciate them in all parts, with such an
aboundance, as cannot be expressed.
Why did I say in all parts? Because their
eies, their eares, their nostrills, their
mouth, their hands, their feete, their
throat, their heart, their liuer, their
lungs, their marrow, their bones, yea
their very bowells, and all their members in general, and each one in particular, shall in common be filled with
                                    such

such an admirable feeling of delight and sweetnes ; that truly the whole man shall be made to drinke of the torrent of Gods pleasure, and inebriated with the plentie of his house.

Psal. 35.

Seuenthly they shall haue that, which all men desire, to wit, long life. For he that liueth well now, shall then liue, as much as God. Whence it is written: The iust shall liue for euer.

Wisd. 5.

There are yet seuen other guifts or dowries (no lesse delightfull then the former) which shall be bestowed vpon the Sainuts in that most happie countrie; which pertaine to the soule, as those alreadie recited belong to the bodie: and these are wisdome, friendship, concord, honour, power, securitia, and ioy.

Eighthly therefore the righteous shall be endewed with so great wisdome in the life to come, that they shall be ignorant of none of those things, which they desire to know. For a good man shalbe replenished with perfect wisdome, which is God, and shall see him face to face. By which sight he shall see the nature

of

of euerie creature, which consisteth
better in God, then in it selfe. For then
the iust shall know all things, which
God hath made to be knowne: aswell
those things, that are past, as those,
which are to come. There all shall be
knowne of euerie one, and euerie one
of all. Neither shall any one be ignorant, of what countrie, nation or
kindred, any one was borne : or
what he hath done in his life time.

Ninthly, there shall be perfect friēd-
ship or amitie in that blessed countrie.
For God, and all others that are good,
do in that manner loue euerie good
man, as that they cannot hate him.
For, as much as euerie one shall loue
himselfe: so much, and so long he shall
loue an other. Neither do I see indeede
how it can be otherwise : especially
seeing all are one bodie of Christ, and
Christ, who is peace it selfe, is the head
of all. Neither shall they with lesse affection be louingly linked together,
then are the members of one bodie
conioyned one to an other. How great
and aboundant thinkest thou will be
thine affection, when thou shalt haue
this

this in poſſeſſion? Howbeit paſſe ouer
theſe things, and contemplate him, by
whome thou haſt arriued to this happines: and thou ſhalt perceiue, that he
doth loue thee more by many degrees,
then thou doſt loue thy ſelfe, and all
others do loue themſelues. And thou
ſhalt loue him more then thy ſelfe,
and more then all others, with a certaine vnſpeakeable ſweetnes.

Tenthly in the next life there ſhall
be moſt perfect concord. For the bodie and ſoule of euerie Sainct, yea all
the Saincts ſhall be of ſo great cócord,
as our eies are in this preſent life. For
like as one eie cannot be turned, whether the other is not alſo turned; but
both are alwayesturned the ſame way:
euen ſo the bodie and ſoule, or that ſo-
cietiè of the iuſt, ſhall be able to deſire
nothing that is different, but ſhall al-
vvayes haue the ſame will. For we ſhall
be one bodie: we ſhall be one Church:
we ſhall (as many I meane as ſhall be
there) be one ſpouſe of Chri. The will
of God will not be different frō thine:
but like as thou ſhalt deſire the ſame
that he doth, ſo he ſhall deſire the ſame
that

that thou dost. For how can the head disagree from the bodie? When therefore thou shalt haue God, and all others agreeable to thy will: then certainely thou shalt desire nothing, which thou shalt not be able to performe.

Eleuenthly the honour of the Saincts shall be surpassing great: in so much, that they shall be called the sonnes of God, yea verie Gods, and shall be the heires of God, and coheires with Christ.

Twelfthly the Sainects shall be so powerfull, as that they shall be able to doe whatsoeuer they will: because they shall haue him that is omnipotent agreable in all things to their will. They therefore (according to S. Augustine) shall be omnipotent of their will, euen as God is of his: For euen as God shall be able to doe whatsoeuer he will by himselfe: so they shall be able to doe, whatsoeuer they will by him: for like as they shall desire nothing, but what he shall be willing to doe: so he shall be willing to doe whatsoeuer they will haue him, and what he will

Gg   haue

haue to be done, muſt of neceſsitie be put in execution. Thus S. Auguſtine. When therefore thou haſt obtained this honour, with the other dowries and prerogatiues before mentioned, I do not ſee with what reaſon thou canſt deſire more. Wherefore when thou shalt be happie through the poſſeſſion of all theſe beatitudes, which we haue recited, wilt thou not thinke thy ſelfe to be rich indeede? Surely, thou wilt anſwere, yes. Goe to then. If in all theſe, according as they are deſcribed, thou shouldeſt liue ſecure but one day onely, doubtleſſe thou wouldeſt re-ioyce. But if this ioy should laſt for a moneth, or for a yeare, or for the whole terme of thy life, what wouldeſt thou doe? Truly the meaſure of this gladnes (as I ſuppoſe) is greater then any one can expreſſe. But yet further, if thou were wholy ſecure and aſſured, that as long as thou liueſt, thou shouldeſt not looſe theſe things by any accident, I omit to ſay, whether thou couldeſt imagin or no, what ioy were wanting vnto thee.

Thirteenthly the Sainⱷs shall haue

most

moſt perfect ſecuritie in the life to
come : in ſo much, that they ſhall haue
whatſoeuer they will , and feare to
looſe nothing thereof. They ſhall be
ſo ſecure neuer to looſe it of their
owne accord, as they ſhall be ſecure
that God, who ſo dearely loueth them,
will not forcibly take it from them:
as they ſhall be ſecure , that there is
nothing of ſufficient power , to ſepa-
rate God and them one from an other.
With what wordes then, can ſo great a
ioy be expreſſed, where ſo great a good
is poſſeſſed ?

Fowerteenthly therefore and laſtly
the Saincts ſhalbe repleniſhed with
vnſpeakeable ioy, and not without iuſt
cauſe, for that they ſhall perfectly obtaine all the aforeſaid parts of bliſſe.
And yet to encreaſe their happines
they ſhall haue an other thing , which
ſhall encreaſe their ioy : for ſithence
euerie one of them ſhall loue an other
as himſelfe ; it is moſt plaine, that he
ſhall reioyce ſo much at his happines,
as at his owne. O how many and how
great ioyes ſhall euerie one obtaine,
who ſhall reioyce at ſo many and ſo

great beatitudes of the Sainɛ̃ts ? But if
he shall reioyce so much in respeɛ̃t of
others, whome he loueth as hiinselfe:
how much will he triumph in respeɛ̃t
of God, whome he loueth aboue himselfe? Verily he will haue ioy within,
and without; ioy aboue and beneath:
ioy on euerie side: full and perfeɛ̃t ioy
in all places.

Now sithence that the iust shall be
blessed through so great felicitie, it
followeth that the wicked contrarily
be wretched through a certaine vny
speakeable miserie. For like as beautie,
agilitie, strength, libertie, health, pleasure, and long life shall cause the iust to
become merrie and ioyfull : so on the
other side, deformitie , lumpishnes,
weakenes, seruitude, sicknes, anguish,
and short life, shall make the mindes
of the wicked to become sad and sorrowfull. Certainely long life which the
iust so much desired that they might
doe the greater good, shall be an intolerable torment to the wicked, for that
they shall haue that, which they so
much detested. For sithence they haue
liued amisse, they cannot liue but by
dying.

dying. Nothing therefore is shorter then that life, to which death isalwaies conioyned.

What shall I say of their wisdome: sithence that as to the iust it shall be a cause of greater ioy and estimation; so to the wicked, whatsoeuer they shall know, shall turne to their sorrow, and confusion?

As for the friendship or amitie of the damned, (if they haue any) it shall turne to their torment. Moreouer God, and all that are good shall so detest and abhorre euerie one that is wicked, that not so much as the sonne shall take pittie of his father, seeing him in torments. They shall be at variance with euerie creature, and euerie creature with them: yea their discord shall be so great, as that their bodie and soule shall alwayes disagree. For both the bodie shall hate the soule, for that at any time it thought vpon euill, and the soule the bodie, for that it accomplished in worke those things which it thought amisse, for all which they are now afflicted with torments.

In steede of honour, which the Saicts shall

shall obtaine , the wicked shall be punished with euerlasting reproach and
confusion. Being likewise so weake
and vnable to helpe themselues, as
that they shall want strength to resist
the wormes that crawle ouer their faces.

Furthermore, as Gods friends shall
be secure neuer to loose that happines
vnto which they are exalted : so the e-
nemies of God shall wholy despaire of
being euer free from those miseries ,
vnto which they are adiudged. In steed
therefore of that eternal ad vnspeakeable ioy and mirth , which the
Sainⅽts shall enioy with the holy Angells in heauen; the wicked shall be af-
fliⅽted with eternal and vnspeakeable
sorrow and anguish in companie of
the diuells , in that hellish lake , that
burneth for euer with fire and brimstone. Thus in effeⅽt writeth that holy.
Father S. Anselme.

Wherefore in that future happines
(according to the assertion of S. Augustine) God shall refresh all the senses
of the blessed with a spiritual and vn-
vnspeakeable delectation and sweet-
                                    nes

nes; sithence that he is to be the obiect of all their senses. For God shall be as a looking glasse to their sight, a harpe to their hearing, honie to their taste, baulme to their smell, as a soft flower to their feeling: who moreouer became man that he might wholy beatifie man in himselfe: and that both the senses of man might be made blessed and delighted in him: that is, the eie of the soule in his diuinitie, and the eie of the bodie in his humanitie: that so our humane nature by him created, might within and without find foode in the same, and be refreshed.

Briefly according to the assertiō of S. Greg. the beautie of iustice is so great; so great likewise is the delight of that eternal light, that albeit we should be permitted to liue or remaine therein for the space of one day onely: yet for the gaining of this short space, we might verie well contemne innumerable dayes and yeares of this life, were they neuer so full of pleasure and contentment. For the Prophet Dauid did not lie when he said to God: *Better is one day* Psal.83. *in thy courts, aboue thousands.*

What

What mortal man (saieth S. Bernard) is able to comprehend how great the felicitie of the Saincts is; to see God, to liue with God, to be of God, who shall be all in all : to haue God, who is the chiefest good : and where the chiefest good is, there is soueraigne felicitie supreme mirth, true libertie, perfect charitie, eternal, societie, and eternal securitie.

This caused S. Augustine to crie out: O ioy aboue ioy, to see God that hath made him, that hath saued him, that hath glorified him, to see the face of his God, who is the chiefest good, the ioy of Angells, and of all the Saincts. For God (according to S. Gregorie) is of that inestimable beautie, that the verie Angells (who in beautie do seuē times surpasse the sunne) desire incessantly to gaze vpon him. There (saieth S. Augustine, speaking of the heauenly Hierusalem) shall arise no malice, no miserie of the flesh: no desire of sinning, no power of offending, but totally mirth, and exultation : these things shall men possesse, being linked in fellowship with the holy Angells.

O my

O my soule, now thou hast heard how great the ioyes are of the righteous, and the excessiuenes of their gladnes, how great likewise the pleasure and contentment of that heauenly citie is. If it were necessarie daily to suffer torments, yea to endure hell it selfe for a long time together, that we might see Christ in his glorie, and be ioyned in fellowship with the Saincts in his heauenly citie: were it not meete (thinkest thou) to sustaine all manner of miserie, that we might be made partaker of so great a good, and of so great felicitie? Let vs therefore (ô my soule) recollect our selues from the hurlieburlie of earthly affections, and expelling the tumults of vnlawfull cogitations from the secrecie of our heart, let vs from thence breath forth sighes through the remembrance of that supernal happines.

Let vs returne to the heauenly citie, in which we are written, and enrolled as citizens of the same. Let vs (as citizens of the Saincts, and God's household seruants, yea as God's heires, and coheires of Christ) consider the felici-

H h   tie

tie of this our famous citie, to the vttermost of our possibilitie. Let vs crie out with the Prophet; O how glorious

Pſal. 86. *things are said of thee ô citie of God, in thee is the dwelling of all those, that are truly glad.* Becauſe thou art built as a place to meete and make merrie, for ſuch as God of his infinite mercie, doth vouchſafe to take vnto himſelfe out of this vale of miſerie.

O happie ioy, and ioyfull happines, to ſee the Sainds, to be with the Saincts, and to be a Sainct: to ſee and enioy God world without end, and longer to, if longer could be imagined. Let vs carefully conſider theſe things, and feruently deſire them, to the end we may ſpeedily be ioyned to the companie of the Sainds in heauen. If thou demaund how this may be done, by what merits or ſuccour: hearken, and thou ſhalt heare. This thing lieth in

Mat.11. the power of the doer, becauſe *the kingdome of heauen ſuffereth violence.* The kingdome of heauen (ô man) asketh no other price then thy ſelfe, it is aſmuch worth as thou art. Giue thy ſelfe therefore, and thou ſhalt haue it. Why

are

art thou troubled and discontent at the price? Christ gaue himselfe, that he might purchasse thee as a kingdome vnto God the Father : giue thou thy selfe after the same manner; to the end thou maiest be his kingdome, and let not sinne raigne in this thy mortal bodie, which is subiect to corruption, but rather let the spirit gouerne, for the obtaining of life euerlasting.

O wretched, and sinnefull soule, if these things which we haue alreadie said of the pleasures and priuiledges of the Sainctes of God, do not moue thee to endeauour (aided with the grace of God)to merit by penance and vertuous actions that eternal beatitude : then feare and tremble : and with feare and trembling consider the dolefull happe and intolerable torments of the damned : that by feare of punishment at least (if not purely for the loue of God, or in hope of that heauenly reward) thou mayest arise from thy sinnefull estate, and be conuerted to our Lord thy God with thy whole heart.

Note therefore, that as among the

damned

damned there is diuersitie of sinnes,
so there shall be diuersitie of paines.
Wherevpon S. Gregorie saieth:There is
(as we may well beleeue) but one general fire : yet it doth not burne all sinners after the same manner.For euerie
one shall feele as much paine as is due
to his sinne: euen as by one and the
same fire; straw, woode, and iron are
burned after a different manner.

This fire is so kindled and enflamed
by the Iudges furie, as that it shall
neede no new fewell, during all eternitie. This made holy Iob to say of a
wicked man. *Fire that is not kinled shall*
deuoure him. Of the grieuousnes of this
fire S. Sebastian (at whose eare an Angell was seene to stand, dictating vnto
him what he should say) gaue this
testimonie : to wit, that there is no
more comparison betweene this sensible fire of ours, and that of hell : then
betweene this our sensible fire, and
that painted vpó a wall. Iudorus likewise saieth : In hell there shall be a
certaine dimme light, to the end, that
the damned may be able to see, that
they may lament:not that they may
there-

Iob 20.

thereby receiue any cōfort. For thofe,
whóme the reprobate do now inordinately affect, they shall then fee with
them in torments : to the end, that
their carnal acquaintance preferred
before their Creator may augment the
paine of their owne wretched eftate,
being condemned before their eies to
the fame punishment.

Heere fome perchance will demand
whether the damned fee the glorie of
the bleffed. To which queftion. S.
Grégorie| maketh this anfwere in his
homelie of the rich glutton. We ought
to beleeue (faieth he) that the wicked
shall fee fome of the iuft in glorie before the laft day of iudgement : to the
end, that feeing them in bliffe, they
may not onely be afflicted through
their owne torments, but likewife at
the good of others. Howbeit the iuft do
alwaies fee the wicked in torments,
that from thence their ioy may encreafe: becaufe they fee the miferie,
which mercifully they haue efcaped,
and thereby giue fo much the greater
thankes to God, by how much they fee
that in others, which they might haue
endu-

endured, if they had beene left to themselues. And the same holy Father saieth in an other place. The open paine of the reprobate shall not diminish the glorie of the blessed : for that the blessed shall there take no pittie of those that are wretched, neither can their mirth be by any meanes diminished. And albeit in the nature of their goodnes they are compassionate, yet then they shalbe conioyned to the iustice of their Creator with so great rectitude, as that they shalbe moued with no compassion towards the reprobate: And Prosper addeth, that then the miserie of children or parents, of husband, or wife, shall in no sort grieue the blessed.

Howbeit the damned shall see the blessed before the day of iudgement, not in that manner, as that they shall know what their glorie is, but onely may perceiue, that they are in inestimable blisse : neuerthelesse they shall be afflicted with enuie, grieuing at the happines of the blessed, of which sight they shall be depriued : and yet their paine by this shall not be diminished, but

but augmented, becaufe they fhall remember the glorie of the bleffed, which they haue feene, at or before the day of iudgement, and this fhall turne to their torment.

Moreouer they fhalbe afflicted in this refpect, for that they fhall fee themfelues deemed vnworthy of that glorie, which is imparted to the elect.

Some likewife are wont to demand, whether the damned fee thofe things, which are done in the world. To this S. Gregorie maketh anfwere in the fecond booke of his moralls, difputing vpon that place of Iob. *Whether his children fhall be noble or vnnoble, he fhall not vnderftand.* Euen as they, which are yet liuing know not in what place the foules of the dead are: fo thofe that are dead, know not what is done in the world after their departure : becaufe the life of the fpirit is farre different from the life of the flefh. Iob 14.

As for the foules of the bleffed, we may be affured, that fithence they inwardly fee the brightnes of almightie God, they are in no fort ignorant of thofe things, which are outwardly

done

done in the world. The good therefore fee what is done concerning their
familie and friends, but with the
wicked it is cleane otherwife. But if
you make this obiection: The glorie
of the bleſſed is more diſtant from the
damned, then thoſe things, that are
done in the world: but they (as you
haue alreadie gráted) do not ſee thoſe
things, that are done in the world; er-
go much leſſe can they ſee the glorie of
the bleſſed. To this I anſwere, that
thoſe things which are done heere in
this world, would not ſo afflict the
damned in hell, if they were ſeene, as
doth the glorie of the Sainds in heaué.
And for this reaſon the things that are
heere done, are not ſhewed to the dāned; but thoſe things onrely, which
may augment their torment.

Some againe will be readie to demand, whether the damned in hell
would wiſh, that all others were partakers with them in the ſame miſeries.
To this I replie: that like as the Saincts
in heauen ſhall abound with moſt perfect charitie: ſo the damned in hell
ſhall be readie to burſt with hatred ād
enuie

enuie. Wherevpon as all things that are
good, shall to the good be a caufe of
gladnes; fo to the wicked whatfoeuer
is good will be a caufe of griefe and
anguish. And for that the felicitie of
the Sainéts, confidered by them, doth
exceedingly afflié them: for this reafon they could wish that all the Sainéts
were in the fame ftate of damnation.
For their hatred shall be fo great, that
they (feeing their owne miferie) shall
likewife enuie at their owne kinsfolke
which through extremitie of hatred
hapneth alfo in this world.

Howbeit they enuie leffe at their
owne friends and quondam acquaintance, then at others; and their forrow
would be greater, if all their kinred
should be damned, and others faued;
then if fome of their kindred were faued. The rich glutton may ferue as an
example to confirme what I fay, who
defired that his brethren might efcape
damnation: for he knew, that it was
likely that fome of thé would efcape:
neuertheleffe he had rather, that they
might not be dáned with others. And
know, that albeit of the multitude of

Luc.16.

I i   the

the damned the paine of each one in particular is encreafed onely, yet the hatred and malice of them all doth encreafe, for that they rather make choyce to be tormented with many, then with one alone.

It may likewife be demanded, whether the dead, (efpecially the damned) shall know or remember thofe things, which they knew, whiles they earft liued in the world. To this I anfwere, that in the damned there shall be a côfideration of thofe things, which formerly they haue knowne, as a material caufe of forrow, and in no forte to delight them. For they shall confider the euills which they haue committed, for which they are damned; and the good workes, which they haue omitted, and by both thefe they shall be tormented.

Know further, that in hell there is a two-fold paine, the paine of loffe, and the paine of feeling. Whereof our Sauiour himfelfe fpake in the Gofpel, saying: *Euerie tree, that yeeldeth not fruit, shall be cut downe, and caft into the fire.* Of the paine of feeling, which is diuerfe,

Mat. 7.

S.

S. Gregorie vpon those wordes of the eighth chapter of S. Mathewes Gospel, *But the children of the kidgdome shall be* Mat.8. *cast out into the exteriour darknes,* saieth thus: In hell there shall be an intolerable cold, an vnquenchable fire, an immortal worme, an vnsufferable stench, palpable darknes, the whippes and scourges of the tormentors, the gastly sight of diuells, the shame or confusiõ of sinnes, the despaire of all goodnes. For to those wretched caytiffs there shall be death without death, failing without failing: because death there doth continually begin, but can neuer end.

The damned therefore (as we may well suppose) shall be full of sorrow and anguish. They shall haue teares in their eies, gnashīg in their teeth, loathsome sauoures in their nostrills, lamentation in their voyces, terrour in their eares, manicles on their hands, fetters on their feete, fire aud heate in all their members. Wherevpon a certaine holy man speaking of hell, made this dolefull description of that woefull place: Hell is a most deadly pit, re-

Ii 2   ple-

plenished with all paines, ãd miseries.
And therefore the Prophet Dauid
cryed out vnto God almightie : *Let not*
the pit shut his mouth vpon me. Because
when hell shall receiue those into it,
that are guiltie of sinne . it is shut vpward, ãd opened downeward towards
the bottome : no chimney or place to
fetch breath shall be left open , the entrance aboue being made fast and firme. *There* (as is written in the thir-
teenth Chapter of the Prophet Isay)
euerie one shall be astonied at his neighbour,
their countenances as faces burnt. Because
(as the Prophet Baruch saieth) *their*
faces are black with the smoke. For that
(as Nahum testifieth) *the faces of them all*
shall be as the blacknes of a pot.

Moreouer the bitternes of the paines
of hell may be gathered by the weeping and gnashing of teeth of the
damned, by the eating of their tõgues,
and blaspheming their Creator, and
diuerse other torments mentioned in
sondrie places of the holy scripture.
For so we read in the 16. chapter of the
Apocalypse of S. Iohn . *They together*
(saieth he *). did eate their tongues for*
paine:

Psal.68.

Isai. 13.

Baruch.
6.

Nahum
2.

Apoc.16

paine : *and they blafphemed the God of*
heauen, becaufe of their paines and wounes.
Yea the paines of hell shall be fo exceeding great, as that the damned defpi-
fing and contemning life (which all
men ordinarily couet) shall heartily
wish for death, which fo many feeke
to auoid. *In thofe dayes* (faieth S. Iohn in
an other place of his Apocalyps) *men* Apoc.9.
shall feeke for death, and shall not find it:
and they shall defire to die, and death shall
flie from them.

Alas (faieth S. Iohn Chryfoftome)
what shall we doe there? what shall we
anfwere ? There shalbe nothing but
weeping, howling, and gnashing of
teeth : and to too late repentance : all
affiftance on euerie fide ceafing, and
paines on euerie fide encreafing, without the leaft hope of comfort or confolation. No others will there occurre to
our fight, but thofe ouglie diuells, by
whome we are tormented: yea, (which
is worfe then any of the things recited) we shall haue no comfort either
of ayre or light. Now being in thefe
diftreffes, how great will be our feare,
and anguish ? how great will be the
gri-

griping, and conuulsion of our members? Certainely no tongue is able to
expresse, what and how great crosses
or calamities shall befall vs in all our
senses.

Concerning the paine of losse, the
same holy Father in an other place
saieth thus. There are many men
(saieth he) that are onely affraid of
hell: howbeit I affirme, that the losse
of eternal glorie and happines is much
more grieuous then hell it selfe: neither is it a wonder, if it cannot be
proued with wordes. For sithence we
know not the felicitie of that future
life, consequently we know not the
miserie that doth entue from the pri-
uation thereof. Howbeit S. Paul that
apparantly knew that future happines, knew likewise that to be depriued
of the glorie of Christ, is the most grieuous torment of all others. We also
shall then know it, when we shall
come to feele it. But we beseech thee,
ô onely begotten sonne of God, that
we may neuer feele the same, neither
let vs euer haue experience of that ir-
reparable paine. For it cannot be expressed

preſſed, how great an euill it is to be
depriued of that vnſpeakeable good.
Hell, and the paine thereof is intolerable: howbeit although any one ſuppoſe infinite hells, yet it is as it were
nothing, in reſpect of the loſſe of that
happie glorie, and of the loue of Chriſt:
to heare him ſay : I know you not :
and to be accuſed, that ſeeing him Mat. 25.
hungrie we haue not fed him. For it is
better to endure a thouſand thunder-
clapps, then to ſee that ſweet counte-
nance of his turned from vs, and his
amiable eie, not daining to looke vpon
vs. Thus S. Chryſoſtome.

Woe be to vs, that doe not thinke of
theſe euills, but remaining ſecure in
our ſluggiſhnes, and neglecting the
care of our ſoules do inceſſantly haſten
towards theſe miſeries.

But peraduenture ſome man will
ſay: It ſeemeth that God is vniuſt, who
puniſheth man eternallie for a mortal ſinne, which oftimes is committed on a ſodaine. Sainct Gregorie pro-
poundeth this queſtion, and in this
máner ſolueth the ſame. I would faine
know (ſaieth he) how it can ſtand
                                      with

with the iuſtice of God ; that ſinne,
which is temporally committed, can
eternally be puniſhed. And he giueth
himſelfe this anſwere. This queſtion
might well be demanded, if the ſtrict
iudge did not conſider men's hearts,
but their wordes. For wicked men
would offend for euer, if they might
liue for euer. For if they could, they
would ſinne euerlaſtingly : For they
ſhew, that they deſire alwayes to liue
in ſinne, who neuer ceaſe to ſinne. It
belōgeth therefore to the great iuſtice
of the iudge, that he neuer want
puniſhment, who in this life would
neuer want fault : and that no end of
reuenge be limited to a wicked man,
who aſlong as he liued, would haue
no end of his ſinne,

An other reaſon why an eternal paine
is due to euerie mortal ſinne, may
be taken from his part, againſt whome
it is committed, who is of infinitie
goodnes and power, to wit God.
Wherevpon the offenſe done againſt
him is worthy of an infinite paine :
becauſe by how much the greater he
is, that is wronged; by ſo much the
more

more seuerely the wrong is to be punished, according to the assertion of Aristotle in his Moralls. S. Iohn Chrysostome is of the same opinion. Euerie iniurie (saieth he) is such, as is the person, to whome the iniurie is done. A small iniurie towards a person of qualitie or estate, is to be esteemed great: and a great iniurie done to one that is base and contemptible, seemeth but little.

Consider all these things (deare Christian reader) with care and attention, and pondering them continually in thy heart, haue a care of thy saluation. Set before thine eies the eternal and intolerable paines of hell : and seeke in time to doe that which is best and most profitable for thy soule. Is it not better to lament and craue pardon for thy sinnes in this world: then to lament in that euerlasting fire without any profit? For in this short space by penance and teares thou maiest merit forgiuenes and comfort.

Lament therefore a little heere, least thou lament there for euer and euer. Humble thy selfe heere, least

K k   thou

thou be humbled there, and caſt into
outward darknes and vnquencheable
fire. Happie is he, who whiles he remaineth in this world, ſtriueth to
make himſelfe worthy with thoſe that
ſhall be worthy at the day of iudgement: contrariwiſe he is moſt wretched, who by ſinning doth make himſelfe vnworthy of the glorie of God.
At that hower a bright cloud ſhall receiue all the Sainǎs vp into heauen: as
for the wicked, the diuells ſhall ſeize
vpon them, and caſt them downe
headlong into that fournace, that burneth for euer with fire and brimſtone.

Iere. 5.

*Who will giue water to my head, and
to mine eies a fountaine of teares ?* that I
may weepe and lament day and night:
and by weeping and lamenting may
obtaine pardon, and ſo be found worthy at the day of our Lord's comming?
Yea let vs all weepe and lament, and
by penance puniſh our ſelues whiles
we liue in this world: for if we be not
afflicǎed heere, we ſhall moſt aſſuredly
be afflicǎed more ſeuerely heereafter.
Why do we not make choice to be afflicǎed heere, that we may reſt there,

and

and obtaine thofe vnfpeakeable ioyes which shall continue for euer? For if we be void of good workes; all things will paffe, and we vndoubtedly shall euerlaftingly perish. No man shall be able to helpe vs at that dreadfull hower; neither father, nor brother, nor fonne, nor friend, nor neighbour, nor any other. How much did the rich glutton lament, and befeech the Patriarch, that he would fend Lazarus to eafe him of his torments? But liften what anfwere Abraham gaue him. *Betweene vs and you*, faid he, *there is fixed a great chaos : that they that will paffe from hence to you, may not, neither goe from thence hither.* So then, although thofe that are in heauen should defire to defcend to thofe that are in hell, yet they shall not be able. How earneftly did the foolish virgins entreat their companions for a little oyle. But heare what they alfo faid. *Leaft peraduenture there fuffice not for vs and you, goe rather to them that fell : and buy for your felues.* Neither could any one bring them into the chamber of the bridegroome. Let vs therefore confidering thefe

Luke. 16.

Mat. 25.

Kk 2   things,

things, haue a care of our selues , and
amend our liues : that liuing heere
worthy of a kingdome , we may both
escape those future paines of damnation , and obtaine life euerlasting,
through the grace and mercie of
Christ Iesus our Lord and Sauiour:
to whome with the Father ,
and the holy Ghost, be all
glorie , honour , and
power, both now and
for euermore.
Amen.

FINIS.

CER-

CERTAINE PIOVS AND
Pathetical verses, shewing (like the two former Treatises) the manifold dangers and miseries of man's life, and the sondrie calamities that ensue at the end thereof.

The Translator to the gentle Reader.

 HE Character of man, his passage heere;
His life, and death, his hopes, and cause of feare:
The operations of his soule, and sense,
The wayes of danger, and of excellence,
Errors of flesh and blood, workes more diuine,
Thoughts that tend vpward, actions that decline:

These

These with their endes, as they are curſt or
    bleſt,
A heere explaned, and at large expreſt.
And albeit in verſe I ſay no more,
Then what in proſe hath beene rehearſt be-
    fore:
Yet if the ſelfe-ſame meate, well varied, proue
More fit to pleaſe his taſte, that doth approue
But as his proper fancie leades him: then
This ſecond change may iuſtifie my pen.
Wordes that in meaſure moue, do ſometimes
    take
With thoſe, that would ſuch ſubiects els for-
    ſake.
Harmonious accents correſpond that eare,
Whoſe paſſion muſt in paſſion all things heare.
I do confeſſe, my aimes are all may know
The fountaine, whence both good and ill do
    flow.
And in that kind it is enough for me,
If that my leaues or lines ſucceſfull be.
Since ſo diuine a worke well practis'd, may
Crowne vs with glorie, and inſtruct the way.

A

A Dolefull Dialogue or *disputation,*
betweene the soule and bodie
of a damned man.

THe gloomie night had her black mantle
    spread,
The canopie of darknes crownd her head.
No noise or murmure with their eccho shrill
Did interrupt her peace, or wrangling fill
The reconciled ayre: the midinghts Queene
Had maskt vp her pale cheekes, they were not
    seene.
The priuie Councel of the Spheares were hid
By the black cloudes, that through the welkin
    rid:
And all the common people of the skies
Kept in the twinckling beames of their bright
    eies.
In this deepe silent darknes, which surroundes
The Hemisphere : and those the vtmost
    boundes
Of his extension, sadlie I retir'de,

                 Vnto

Vnto my quiet cell. My senses tir'de,
A drousie dulnes so mine eies posse'st,
That I bequeathd my wearie limmes to rest.
Scarce had I recollected or suruaid
My late diurnal cares, scarse was I laid:
When loe a slumbring heauines did seaze
My wearie powres, glad to embrace their ease.
In which my sleeping fancie was enforst
To vieue a wandering spirit late diuorst
From the sad owner: and close by appeares
All pale and wan, quite sullied, drown'd in
    teares.
As they together stood, the Soule (whose
    moanes.
So deepely were exprest, the ayre euen
    groanes.)
With bitter repetitions sadlie shewes.
Her griefe, and thus expostulates her woes.

The Soule.

VNhappie Flesh, whie didst thou prostrate
    soe
Thy selfe? (now base) adorn'd not long agoe,
With honour, high command, with riches
    store,
With followers, friends, with seruants to adore
Thy then resplédent greatnes, which was such,
                                            Thou

Thou feltst no worldlie want, but hadst too
    much.

Where now are all those glorious shadowes?
    where

Thy flock of fawning minions? Do they feare
To touch thy ruins ? and (like rattes) forsake
Thy false foundation, when they saw it shake?
See now the vertue of thy choice, that tooke
Such as haue lou'd thy fortune, thee forsooke.

Poore summer-flies, that by the sunne-shine
    thriue,

And scorne those dead, whome they ador'd
    aliue.

What doth the glorie of those buildings hide,
In triumph which proclaim'd their maisters
    pride ?

So richly furnisht, and so stronglie built,
So neatlie pollisht, and so fairely guilt.

Do these refuse thee house-roome and haue
    sent

Thee to this narrow cage , where thou art
    pent

Euen from the verie ayre ? O fruitlesse cost !
Enioyd so little, and so quickly lost.

To what end serues such choice of goodlie
    towers ,

When a poore coffin thy proud feete em-
    bowers ?

            L   Or

Or thofe thy fpatious roomes, fince thou muſt
    dwell,
Within this vault, or deeper farre in hell?
Can thy reuenue, nor thy treaſure winne,
Nor roome nor priuiledge to cleanſe thy ſinne?
Theſe all haue left thee, now thy glorie's
    ſhronke,
And thou haſt nothing, but thy naked tronke.
Caſt on a beere, empriſond in a cheſt,
Confinde into a caue, with wormes oppreſt.
For euer loſt, eternallie contemn'd,
To neuer dying torments ſtill condemn'd.
No helpe, no eaſe, no hope, no reſpit there
Can intermiſſion giue thy paines or feare.
Heere thou art ſtraightned in too cloſe a
    roome,
To worke oppreſſions by thy partial doome.
Thou canſt not now a ier ke of craft deuiſe,
Or plot that proieɕ can thy foes ſurpriſe.
Heere are no myſteries, no liggs of ſtate,
No ſtratagems, that can thee hence tranſlate.
Nor canſt thou heere ſupplant, or poiſon
    thoſe,
That to thy endes in oppoſition goes.
Such thy polluted aɕes ſo horrid, fowle,
Haue damned thee; and me thy wretched
    ſoule.
Alas I had a farre more noble birth:

                            Stampt

Stampt with my makers image (wretched
  Earth)
T'was thou betraidst vs, which wouldst not
  fore-cast,
Those bitter paines we must for euer taste.
Corruption of thy nature made thee blinde,
Thou neither cared'st to seeke, nor wouldst
  thou finde
The way to that eternal blisse, which might
In death haue crown'd, and liuing kept thee
  right.
Those inward motions of a natiue feare,
Which flesh and blood doth from the cradle
  beare,
Could not but touch thy heart, and make thee
  know
The end, to which such lewd affections goe.
Thou could'st not choose but vnderstand the
  state
Of those poore wretched soules, that (ah) too
  late
Repent their foule contempt, and want of
  grace,
Which hurles the headlog to that cursed place,
Where neuer dying torments, endlesse griefe
Gnawes on their bowells, hopelesse of reliefe.
Why then betimes didst thou not seeke to
  shunne

The

The errors, which thou knewſt had thoſe vndonne?

But thou ran'ſt on ſecurely without ſenſe,
Or leaſt compunction of ſo foule offenſe:
Borr'wing a libertie to ſinne by courſe,
Without diſlike, repentance, or remorſe.

Thrice happie hadſt thou beene, if from the
wombe,
Thou hadſt beene carried to the hungrie
tombe.

Time, and the length of life hath nothing
wonne
But that in thee, which hath thee quite vndonne.

And tis no wonder when thou wert aliue
Thou knew'ſt no goodnes: and did'ſt ſo con-
triue,
That mine was powreleſſe to controule thy
will,
Which headlong ranne to act all kindes of ilł.

Nay (which was worſe) thou didſt not onely
act,
But hauing donne, didſt glorie in the fact.

Canſt thou in iuſtice then thy ſentence blame,
That liud'ſt in deedes of darknes, ſinne, and
ſhame?

Whereby we ſuffer now this cruel paine,
Which as it ſtill renewes, muſt ſtill remaine.

                                        What

What now auailes thy purchases engrost?
What those same structures, built with so much
    cost?
To what end serue thy Iewells, massie plate,
Thy vaine delightes, thy ioyes adulterate?
Thy glorious outside, and Maiestick looke?
Haue these thy cursed fortune all forsooke?
Where be those ornaments that cloath'd thy
    pride,
Thy suites, that with proud May their colours
    vide?
Those purer vestments, white as swannie
    plumes,
Those Aromatick drugges, those sweet per-
    fumes?
Doth now thy house his forelorne tenant
    please?
Me thinke, the thought of this should thee
    disease.
What thing of worth doth now to thee belong?
Thine eies are blinde, and motionlesse thy
    tongue:
Thy limmes are withered; and thy heart
    growne cold,
Doth neither blood, nor vital spirit hold.
They sense is lost, and thou must senslesse be,
Till revnited thou partake with me.
Thy memorie is hatefull, and thy name

A by word made of scorne, disgrace, and
    shame.
All that thou didst ignobly scraping gaine
By fraud, oppression, briberie, and paine;
Spending so many dayes, so many yeares,
To make thy surfet more, and more thy cares,
Pale death in one poore minute hath bereaft,
And basely naked thee their maister leaft.
The flower, whose blossomes withering drop
    to ground.
Hath seldome times a friendlie pittie found.
The winter come, the glorious summer done,
The leafe-lesse tree the passenger doth shunne.
The rising Sunne the Easterne world adores.
If once declining, few or none implores.
Such thy condition : scarce thy storie's told.
Thy wedlocks teares grow trie, her sorrow cold
Nor may thy hopes vnto thy parents flee,
They tend their vintage, lands, not thinke
    on thee.
Thy store of treasure, which thou keeptst
    vnspent,
Make but thine heire more nimbly thee la-
    ment.
Yet I scarce thinke thy widow, & thy child,
Will giue fine acres of their poorest field
To ransome vs, that being thus bereaft
Of life: are vnto endlesse torments leaft-

                    Alas

Alas that kind of loue is banisht hence,
And hath forsaked this our clime long since.
While in her Virgin truth Religion spread
Her sacred wings triumphant; all were lead
With one sweet vniforme consent , which
　　　taught ,
That prayers and oblations ransomes brought
To those distressed soules, that do remaine
Confind, vntill they can their freedome gaine.
Then men did striue by goodnes to make
　　　sure
A real friendship, that might still endure.
The liuing then their suffrages did make
For those dead friends, whome dying we for-
　　　sake.
Since the beleefe of Purgatorie faild,
Both heau'n and hell ate thought to be entaild
By a predestin'd power: this Tenet shewes
How neere to Atheisme such religion growes;
Which if but one degree it farther fall,
May thinke there is no heau'n, nor hell at all.
Art thou so soone by those in nature tide,
So fully slighted? Doth thy goodnes slide
Into the graue vnpittied? Is thy name,
Left to the world vngarded? whiles thy shame
Diuulged flies abroad, in the complaint
Of those loose tongues, that to the life do paint
Thine insolence, oppression, furie, pride,
　　　　　　　　　　　　　Tyran-

Tyraunick actes, with luſt and murder dide?
Nay (to a noble death which is farre worſe)
Thy memorie they do both loath and curſe.
Now fleſh thou ſeeſt the world, and maiſt ob-
 ſerue,
How it doth thoſe, that fawne vpon it, ſerue.
A meere impoſture, falſe, and counterfeit,
That harbours miſcheiſe, malice, and deceit.
With miſeries repleniſht, deepely, ſtain'd
With poiſon; which hath vs for euer maim'd.
The fatal enemie that firſt betrai'd
Mankind, ſo cumingly-his baites hath lai'd:
That it requires a warie watchfull eie,
To ſhunne his ſnares, or his enticements flie:
This yet to little (he is ſo prepar'd)
Without ſupernal grace, and Angells guard.
Theſe in thy life thou didſt not ſeeke to winne,
Which makes thee feele the iuſt reward of
 ſinne.
How are thy glorious robes ſo much trans-
 form'd,
Thy cloake vnto a winding ſheete is torn'd,
ſcarce worth the wearing, tis ſo ſtraight and
 ſcant;
Me thinkes thou roome to breath or moue
 doſt want.
Haſt thou no other weed thy ſhame to hide,
That had'ſt ſo many to improue thy pride?
     O wret-

O wretched state of greatnes! Which no more
Enioy'st one myte, of all thou hadst before.
Heere are no poore, that do their tribute bring,
To offer vp to thee so poore a thing.

Heere are no Sycophants, whose oylie tongues
Can sooth thee vp in thy apparant wrongs.
No prostitute, no base obsequious slaue,
To runne at thy command: alas thy graue
Hath ta'ne all from thee, but alone thy guilt
And punishment : for all those blessings spilt.

The suitors flock not heere , with purses
    cramm'd
To buy thy fauour : they beleeue thee damn'd
For such thy rapine and extorsion, which
Did begger thousandes, for to make thee rich:
Yet death , thou seest, hath made thee poorer
    farre,
Then those on earth which liuing poorest are.

And know the time will come thou must haue
    part,
Though yet thou be insensible of smart.
All holy writes agree, that thou shalt share
The punishment of my distresse and care.

Though for a time thou do concealed sleepe,
Though wormes consume thee , and the graue
    do keepe
Thy flesh and bones, dissolu'd to verie dust :
Yet be assur'd, that rise againe thou must,

M m   Not

Not to thy former iollitie or ſtate,
Of which thou wert poſſeſt and ſeiz'd of late:
But to a world of euerlaſting griefe,
That hath no end, no reſpit, no reliefe.
But longer now I may not ſtay, farewell,
I know, thou know'ſt not what to anſwer well.

The Bodie.

SCarce had the ſoule concluded, when the
    Flesh
Rows'd it ſelfe vp, as if it liu'd afresh:
And though it were key-cold, and bloodleſſe
    dead,
It ſtill retaines thoſe ſymptomes, liuing ſead
Its looſe affections: which did make it ſtriue
T'o expreſſe it ſelfe, as if it were aliue.
Yet that ſad melancholy ſhape transform'd,
Occaſion'd that this task was ſo perform'd,
As if it were in deepeſt paſſion fixt:
With griefe and anger equally commixt.
With ſighes and groanes, the herbingers of
    woe,
It askt, who t'was, that had reuil'd it ſoe?
And ſeeing none but this ſad ſhadow by,
In hollow noates, doth make this ſharpe replie,
Why ſtand'ſt thou mute (my ſpirit) ſuffering
    thus

                Vniuſt

Vniust aspersions, that are cast on vs?
Thou maist with pregnant arguments defend,
Though some be true , yet they too much
    transcend,
That soly do impose the guilt of all
Vnto the bodie, that is apt to fall.
I do confesse my weaknes was misled ,
And fond desires my proper fancie fed :
The goodnes of the mind I did abuse,
And for the truth did willfull errours choose.
I not denie, I temporiz'd, and flew
From good, and did the worser part poursue.
Yet if the Soule entic'd the Flesh to stray,
It was her fault, I could not but obey.
Alas, my composition was of earth,
A sullid substance: adde to this, my birth
Was tainted: our first father Adam's fall
By his transgression hath betrai'd vs all :
From whence a strong innated passion springs,
Which loose desires, corrupt affections brings;
And humane nature is procliue to ill,
Although it haue the freedome of its will.
What proper motiue then, that's purely good
Can we expect to flow from flesh and blood?
The little riuelets, and siluer brookes
(Like curled snakes) do with their winding
    crookes
Runne swiftlie on, vntill some dam or bay

Hinder

Hinder their swift progression, stop their way,
Which vncontrowled, to the Ocean hies,
Where all their sweetnes failes, and vertue
    dies :
So doth the current of our Nature runne
To that great gulph, in which we are vndonne.
And though it circkling make a kind of shew,
As if it would to some rich fountaine goe:
Yet if the soule do not withstand its course,
It still runnes on, and doth its passage force
Into the brynie depth, where once being
    drown'd,
Its former goodnes can no more be found.
Alas, where is the strength, the fort that
    keepes ?
When as the watch, and wretched gardian
    sleepes ?
Why doth the soule vnto the flesh giue way,
Since that the flesh the soule doth still betray?
He that the treason knowes, yet Traytor tries,
Suffers in iustice, if betraid he die's.
Admit this structure of fraile flesh and blood
Were (as we may suppose it) pure and good:
Say that their proper gard might well oppose
The threatning danger of so cruel foes;
T'were indiscretion yet to leaue them soe,
That they should into any hazard goe :
Since, if the soule relinquish her commands,

Her

Her safetie in an equal hazard stands.
What thing at best is wretched sensual man?
A bubble; shadow, and his life a spanne.
A flow'er, that withering fades, a breath that
    flies,
A way vnseene, a plant that quicklie dies.
A peece of meere corruption, fairely cloathd
With flesh and blood, to sinne and shame
    betroathd.
A little sicknes, or a slender wound
In his least lymme, his being doth confound.
How many maladies, diseases fell
Do in the center of his bodie dwell?
How many fatal chances do attend
His progresse? which doth oft vntimely end
His pilgrimage, when it is scarce begunne,
And leaues him in the pride of yeares vndone.
If we the bodie leaue, and sift the minde,
We there a chaos of distraction finde.
Affections loose, and passions stronglie bent,
Which nought but straines of their owne wayes
    recent.
Is this the character doth truly speake
Poore man? alas is he so faint and weake
In mind and bodie? Doth his nature proue
A traytor to it selfe? and doth it moue
Suggestions, onely to delight the sense,
Wauing those workes of greater excellence?
                    Where

Where is the guide that may direct and gard
Him from the dangers, that are so prepar'd?
When the almightie power so great, so good,
Aboue conceipt, had giuen to flesh and blood
Life and a being, he vnites a soule,
And gaue it power to maister and controwle.
Their motions, if they struggle or rebell,
Shee by her actiue vertue might repell.
Ouer the vigour, strength, the will, the sense,
Shee, shee alone, hath the preheminence.
Whence comes it then, that mine should be so
 free,
Yet I lesse faultie must condemned be?
The world a Syren sweet, and so too strong,
With golden dreames did me oppresse and
 wrong:
The diuel did with all his force conspire,
Mine actions might concurre with my desire:
When two such seeming friendes did leade
 me on,
How could I choose but yeeld, and be vndonne?
Whiles thou (my soule) did'st giue a free
 consent,
And thine assistance to my errours lent.
If God created thee (as thy pretence
Doth challenge) great and good, t'was thine
 offence.
To his similitude he framed thee ,

                                   Which

which but thine hand-maid hath ordained me.
Thou we t the Ladie, he so righly fraught
With reason , iudgement : that thou mightst
    haue taught
My stubborne heart : why didst thou then giue
    way
I should be thus betrai'd, and made a prey?
It is not iust these faults vpbraidinghe
Thou from thy selfe transferre, and cast on me.
With mild inducements , counsel sweet and
    graue ,
Thou mightst haue wonne me to haue beene
    thy slaue :
With waightie reasons, and instructions sound
Me to obedience thou hadst firmely bound.
If these had faild, and thou thy aymes hadst
    mist,
Thou shouldst haue still gone on , and not
    desist.
When I growne proud began to domineere
Thou shouldst haue vs'd thy powre, and beene
    austere.
Thou shouldst haue pin'd , and mortified me
    well,
When thou beheldst me readie to rebell.
With strict prescriptions thou should'st haue
    enform'd
The coming danger, and haue kept me arm'd.
                                    But

But thou well pleas'd , whiles I at random
   runne ,
Sat'st still and silent, till I was vndunne.
Nay (which is more) when I was loosely bent,
Thou pawn'st thy selfe, to further mine intent.
Why didst thou not this charge impose before,
That when I sin'd, I might haue sin'd no more?
Had'st thou in time so smart a lecture read,
Repentant teares had me to newnes lead.
If thou in time had'st me instructed right,
I had become a perfect Conuertite.
Now that I am of sense and life bereft ,
And (past all hope) vnto these torments left:
Now that condemn'd, I cannot mercie pleade,
Nor mediators find to interceade;
Now thundring lowdlie , thou dost me ac-
   cuse,
As if my errors might thy faultes excuse.
Would' thou thine owne conditiõ sift and trie,
Searching the depth, where our offenses lie:
Thou there might'st find thy proper guilt , as
   gret
As mine , whome fondly , thou dost thus
   entreat.
I sin'd, but by the course of nature forc'st,
Thou vnconstrained hast thy selfe diuor'st
From those rich ioyes, which so triumphant be,
Crown'd with the glorie of eternitie.

                     Thou

Thou didst commit a double sinne in this,
Thou gau'st me way, and didst thy selfe amisse.
The flesh without the soule doth nought
    contriue,
Tis by her ministrie it doth suruiue.
Vnlesse by her fresh vigor it be cheer'd,
It dies to goodnes, and is then endeerd
To those bewitching blandishments, that haue
A wofull ending, and a cursed graue.
Nor doth the flesh the way to ill discerne,
Vntill it from the willing spirit learne:
When it but acts her pleasure, which approues
The flesh quite dead, but whē the spirit moues.
Who's then more faultie, shee that is the cause,
Or he at second hand that breakes the lawes?
Shee knew the error, that went hand in hand
With me, that did obey, had no command.
Shee could discerne, and iudge the fact vnfit,
Whiles but by her, I could not censure it.
How comes it then, that when the fact is
    done,
I am the subiect, that t'is cast vpon?
If it be iust we to the man impute
The Maisters errors, if he execute:
If there be reason one do beare the blame
Where two are guiltie of the sinne and shame:
If that the bridegroome must be thought
    vniust,

N.n

When

When that his spouse proues false, and wrongs
    his trust;

The soule may then no question guiltlesse
    stand,

Although the flesh do worke but her commãd.

Shee may be free, that had an equal share

In these transgressions, which so heinous are.

But this position holdes not, those must beare

Their owne and proper guilt, that guiltie were:

The law of lawes doth not with those dispense,

That tainted are, with the selfe-same offense.

If thou hadst meant to keepe thy selfe secure,

How e're I err'd, thou should'st haue beene still
    pure:

And when so many dangers great appear'd,

Thou sat'st at helme and should'st haue better
    steard.

Thou shouldst haue let thine anchor swiftlie
    slide,

When thou beheldst so strong a wind, and tide:

Since thou hadst power that might the flesh
    controwle,

In thy neglect thou sinn'dst, beleeue it, Soule.

But tis in vaine to question and dispute,

Or to each other these our faults impute.

Both time and hope are vanisht now and gone,

Which had vs sau'd, being sooner thought
    vpon.

The

The hungrie wormes do on my bowells prey,
Then soule be gone; I may no longer stay.

The Soule.

Like to the motion of some moorish ground,
Within whose hollow vaines the ayre hath
found
His passage stopt, which doth a rupture force,
Tearing those entrailes, that withstand his
course;
Vntill at last the whole foundation shake,
And each part doth with agitation quake:
Such were the mouings of the troubled soule,
Seeing the flesh presume thus to controwle
The passages of that her iust complaint:
Shee quiuiring shakes, and growes extremely
faint,
Till that the whirle-wind of her inward paine
Dispeirst it selfe, and did with torment straine
A new eruption: whence did swiftly flie
A second charge, in a more sharpe replie.
Perhaps, proud Flesh, thou think'st with lan-
guage faire,
Thou canst thy selfe excuse, and me empaire:
But I will firmely proue, and plainely show,
Thine vniust taxes I can ouerthrow.
Tis not thy wordes so false and steept in gall

Can

Can taint the spirit with the guilt of all
Thou hast committed, whiles thou wert aliue:
From which fond ground thou vainely dost
    deriue
These tearmes, that in so harsh a style repell
Those well knowne errors, in thy heart that
    dwell.
Thus much to truth, I freely do confesse,
My dutie bad me tame thy wilfulnes.
It was my part to ouersee and guide
Thy loose disorder, and insulting pride.
But how could I attaine to compasse this,
Thou being resolu'd to act what was amisse?
How oft wooed I thee with my liquid teares,
Whiles thou didst close thine eies, and stop
    thine eares?
With watches, fastes, with penances I came,
Fully resolu'd thy reprosie to tame.
With gentler inspirations, motiues sweet
How oft did I suggest, how oft entreat?
How many times did I contest and striue,
Thy dying sparkes of goodnes to reuiue?
Whiles carelesse thou didst to thy pleasures flie,
Lead by the motions of thy wandering eie.
And like a bosome foe didst slylie claime.
More soueraigntie, then such a slaue became.
Those miracles of nature, lampes of life,
Chiefe mouers of delight, and cause of strife.
             How

How did they rowle, and wander to and fro,
Like two loose courtisans, that court and wooe
Each obiect new, that might delight the sense,
As if it were some thing of excellence?
Sending impressions to the willing heart,
Who soone consents to yeelde, and take their
    part.
The sentinells thou hadst to gard thy braine,
How did they harbour, cherish, entertaine
Those ayrie foes, that with their sugred layes,
Stroue to betray thy peace, and end thy dayes?
Into their hollow concaues;, circkled round.
Treason flew in, that did the soule confound:
Thow badd'st it wellcome, and receaud'st it soe,
That it did soone thy iudgement ouer throw.
Those louely braches, brother twins, prepa'rd
To be on either side the bodies gard:
Those that do labour, feede, preserue, defend
The tree, from which they spring, and did de-
    cend;
Those that were giuen thee for a vertuous vse,
Thou didst embrue in blood, and still abuse
With wanton touches, and oppressions foule,
Which did the flesh defile, corrupt the soule.
The organ of the voyce, the instrument
That doth expresse the meaning, and intent
Of mans conceptions, lifting him aboue
The ranke of other creatures, which do moue
                Their

Their tongues with a confuſed noyſe,
   whiles he
Brings forth his accents full of harmonie,
Thou mad'ſt the baud to thy luxurious endes,
To wrong whole kingdomes , and betray thy
   friendes.
To waue thoſe other partes, that fitlie matcht,
The bodie, that had ſuch infection catcht.
Let me ſuruay thy cabinet within,
Where thou didſt breed, and foſter vp thy ſinne:
Vpon that braſen table we may finde
A cóſcience larger then thy boundleſſe minde.
What man in anger did thy paſſion ſpare ?
What woman in thy luſt didſt thou forbeare?
What foule oppreſſion didſt thou ſhame to
   vſe ?
What deed of darknes did thy heart refuſe ?
When thou reſolu'dſt a miſchiefe foule and
   great,
Could then the ſting of conſcience thee
   entreat?
When thou to rapine, or to blood wert bent,
Could thy black conſcience croſſe thy baſe
   intent?
When in thy greatnes thou in fauour ſtood,
For goodnes did thy conſcience ere doe good?
But why do I to thee of conſcience ſpeake,
Tha.ne're hadſt any? or if one, ſo weake,
            Thou

Thou couldſt not feele his motion, which did
   moue
Like to the pulſe, the pangs of death doth
   proue.
Thine inward being was ſo void of ſenſe,
At pleaſure thou couldſt with thy ſinns diſ-
   penſe.
Nor didſt thou reſt, when each part did gan-
   grine,
With this foule leproſie and ſinne of thine:
But thou muſt me inueigle, me betray,
To march with thee along the ſelfe-ſame way.
To yeeld to pleaſure, and to ſerue the world,
Which hath me thus into this horrour hurld'.
I know I was too faultie, twas my ſinne,
To be thy maiſtreſſe, and not hold thee in.
But thou betraid'ſt me with a glorious baite,
Which was not as it ſeem'd, but conterfeit.
Nor would'ſt thou leaue me, but importune
   ſtill,
Till I enforc't, was ſubiect to thy will;
Which adds to thy diſorder, makes the skarre
More viſible, and more enormious farre.
When that the heart is tainted and rebells,
It little time in his obedience dwells;
Nor is it with the breach of faith content,
Or with contempt of dutie doth repent:
But in a foule progreſſion onward goes,

                        Vntil

Vntill it doth all hope of goodnes loose.
It is not then content with places high,
Vnlesse it gaine a chiefe soueraignitie.
Such was thy state (proud flesh) when thou
    didst cast
Off thine obedience, and didst freedome tast:
Thou wert not satisfied in making me
The loose companion of thy treacherie:
But thou must needes vsurpe a greater power,
That must my iurisdiction quite deuoure:
Making the soule at thy deuotion stand,
As if shee were a slaue, without command.
When thou hadst none to curbe thee, or con-
    trowle,
Thou then flew'dst out as if thou had'st no
    soule:
All things seem'd lawfull, which thy lawlesse
    will
Resolu'd to act, though they were n'ere so ill.
Nought came amisse that did thy fancie feed,
Though it the depth of mischiefe did exceed.
Thy vertue (like a snake in winter) kept
Her selfe deepe buried, where benumm'd shee
    slept.
Like to the limme a dull-dead palsie chilles,
Whose emptie vaines no vital spirit filles,
Feeles neither touch nor lancing, skarre, no
    wound,

Whiles

Whiles it remaines infesterd, and vnsound :
So far'd it with thy heart, whose inward cell
Was tainted with the Lethargie of hell :
It had no sense of those so cruel blowes,
The soule that wounded , and their venim
  showes.
They were so deepe, so fatal, and so wide,
No huing goodnes could their paines abide.
Sinne is a marchandise, that who so bues ,
Trades vpon trust, but there the danger lies :
The pay day comes , the debter poore con-
  temn'd
Lies in the gayle, for euer there condemn'd.
The pettie chapman trades but on retaile ,
And for small summes doth hope to find his
  baile.
The greater marchant that doth all engrosse,
Suffering a shripwrack, doth lament his losse :
But all in vaine, when he to late hath found,
That with his purchasse he himselfe is drown'd.
This instance fitlie may on him reflect,
To please his sense, who doth his soule neglect ;
He deales with sinnes by whole-sale, swallow's
  all ,
That in the power of wit or action fall :
Till at the last the Tyrant death doth bring
Him, and his luggage all, before the King,
The king of kings, where he a captiue stands,

Arraign'd

Arraign'd for breach of thofe his high com-
    mands.
There is he charg'd with his difcordered acts,
Corrupt proceedings, and vniuft compacts.
There do his deedes, and verie thoughtes ap-
    peare
Before his face, with horrour, shame, and feare.
There all the ftorie of his life is read,
No point forgotten, loft, conceald, or hid.
He cannot pleade to his inditement. Why?
His guilt apparant none can iuftifie.
He cannot alter, or inuert the fenfe
Of that ftrict law, muft cenfure his offenfe;
Nor can he fauour hope, or mercie craue,
That fought it not, till he was in the graue.
What can he then expect, or what alleage,
May ftop the fentence of fo iuft a Iudge?
Alas a treafon and a finne fo foule
Hath not a hope, that may preferue the foule.
Boud faft in chaines, fuch chaines as neuer burft
Adiudg'd to die the death, of deathes the worft.
Caft in the fire, a fire that fcortching burnes,
Yet n'ere confumes, nor vnto ashes turnes.
Whipt, fcortcht, reuiled, mangled in each part,
Such is the end of fuch a traytrous heart.
This is the fatal period of all thofe,
That for the world, do their faluation loofe.
This is the doome, that fot fuch pleafures vaine
                    Suffers

Suffers for euer that infernal paine.

See heere, proud flesh, behold thy present
    state,

The end of all they ioyes adulterate.

Thinke with thy selfe how happie hadst thou
    beene,

If thou such greatnes had'st not knowne, nor
    seene.

Had'st thou despis'd those sweet alluring
    traines,

Kept thy selfe deafe from those enchaunting
    straines:

We had not thus beene tortur'd for our sinnes,

That n'ere shall end, although it now begins.

But the faise world surpri'zd thy heart by
    stealth,

And promist ages of continuing health.

The tyrant death thou didst not know, nor
    feare,

Nor would'st thou of the least affliction heare,

Till thus deluded, at the last thou fell

From thy great height, into the depth of hell.

Poore wretched man is fool'd on earth,
    whiles he

Th'approaching danger will not know, nor
    see:

Whome with her flattering smiles the world
    innerues,

And

And (like a maister worke-man) most ob-
    serues:
It deepliest him , and first of all deceaues,
And for his honour putrefaction leaues:
A food for vermin, turn'd to baser dust,
Such is the end of those, which in it trust.
Like to the skilfull Druggist, that resolu'd
To poyson some great man, hath oft inuolu'd
Within his working braine the readiest way,
And surest, how he may obtaine his pray;
Infuseth nectar in his potion strong,
As if it were a cordial, to prolong
The life , he meanes to ruine , till the taste
Being thus betray'd, the vitall spirits waste.
And at the last the tainted bodie dies
And spotted o're with blaines of venome lies:
The Diuel so, that ma'ns destruction seekes,
The couert way to worke his malice, likes:
Guilding his tenders, mixing those his drinkes
With sweetest mildew, while the poyson sinkes
Downe to the bottome, and remaines vnseene,
Till that the greedie sense haue swallowed in
His owne perdition; which doth follow soone,
Thus wretched mã is cooz'ned, and vndonne.
But peace no more: Accursed flesh , thou now
Maist those thy former errors trulie know,
Although in vaine , but to encrease thy griefe,
Which can no pittie winne, or find reliefe.

                                    I must

I must away, hearke my tormentors houle
Their yelling summons, to me damned soule.

The Bodie.

THe Flesh did listen to this sad discourse,
   Which fully ended, makes it reinforce
Its owne Apologie; but yet exilde
Its former heat : it now growes farre more
   milde,
Keeping a fitter method, which thus spake
Its dolefull passions , which its heart-strings
   brake:
Whiles this dead carcasse breath'd and did pos-
   sesse
Those spirits, which do liuing creatures blesse;
I had possessions plentie, treasures store,
Powre to command, and be obay'd; nay more,
I could both raise, and raze, as I thought best :
Castells, and kingdomes seem'd at my behest.
I could aduance, enrich, my minions raise,
That would my humour feed, my bountie
   praise.
In wealth, in honour, pleasures , vaine
   delightes,
I past the wearie day , and sullen nightes.
What e're the sese could wish, or gold obtaine,
My purse, or friendes did in an instant gaine.

                                        My

My wil was vncotrowl'd, obserul'd my doome,
How could I then suspect, or feare a toombe
Should cloister vp this great commanding
        powre,
And in an instant all my pride deuoure?
Vpon the present times I did reflect,
But those to come I wholie did neglect:
Such meditations seemed too seuere,
That fill'd my trepid vaines with restlesse feare.
Like to the theefe, that sacrilege committs,
I did my braines employ, bestirre my witts,
To compasse mine intentions ; and scarce
        knew
The iust reward to such offences due:
Till at the last I was vn'wares surpris'd,
And felt those torments, I before despis'd.
Such is the end of those designes, that be
Followed at heeles with their owne treacherie.
Now I perceiue no money, honour, strength,
Or knowledge addes a minute to the length
Of those few dayes, that vnto man are told,
And do so many hazards great enfold.
Physitians cordialls, antidotes are vaine,
Earth must to earth, death will the triumph
        gaine.
All flesh is mortal; man but a meere slaue,
To nature, fortune, sicknes, and his graue.
But (ah, alas) why do I this relate?

                                    An

An after-witts experience comes too late.
Condemned prisoners so at their farewell
The cause of their misfortune sadlie tell:
Yet without hope of life, or longer stay,
Then it shall please the deathes-man to giue
     way.
Yet once more soule in answere of thy charge,
Let me thus farre my selfe, and truth enlarge.
Christ may rebuke vs (I confesse he doth)
But not condemne, in equal merit, both.
Who so hath common sense may this com-
     prize,
Which law commandes, experience testifies.
The greater fault to thee is iustlie due,
If thou obserue those proofes, that heere ensue,
He that is trusted most, is deepest ti'de,
In equal measure carefull to abide,
To leuel iustlie an exact account,
So that his debt do not his stock surmount:
Keeping a correspondense faire and iust
With his proportion, that did him entrust,
Or at the least he should most carefull be,
From carelesse losse to be secure and free.
To thee God gaue a puritie of sense,
Wit, vnderstanding, reasons excellence:
A iudgement to suruay, to sift, to trie
The good from ill, though it obscured lie.
A way to know, a memorie to keepe

Diuine

Diuine instructions, and those precepts deepe,
Which with repentant teares may man recall
If he by frailtie into errors fall.
What was the end, this treasure to thy trust
Was giuen? Was it, that the sway of lust,
Of pride, or any other sensual sinne
Should ouer-rule thee, and precedence winne
Before those graue discerning faculties,
Which in the soule of man alone arise?
No no: those blessings of aboundant grace
Were granted, thou should'st honour, not
    deface
His glorious goodnes that hath fullie blest
Man, onely man with so rich guifts possest.
Wit to elect, and reason to discerne,
Iudgement to choose, determine and to learne
The way to his perfection: knowledge fit
To guide the senses, and instruct the wit.
All these were giuen thee, but to this effect
Thou shouldst my foote-stepps guide, mine
    eies direct.
But thou too carelesse, and remisse, wert lead
To giue my will the raines, my passions head.
Like an indulgent mother, whose sick sonne,
Shee, with too fond a care, so doates vpon;
That rather then he should with dressing crie,
Vucur'd, vnsau'd, shee suffers him to die:
Such was thy follie, when the flesh had ta'ne
       The

The deepe infection, which muſt work its
    bane.

Thou ſoothedſt it, and ſcarce wouldſt touch
    the ſore,

Till it ſtill inward feſterd more and more.

By this fond dotage, and neglect vncur'd;

In ſteed of paine the bodie death endur'd.

Nor didſt thou thoſe excurſions lewd con-
    troule,

Tis then moſt cleare, thou art more guiltie,
    ſoule,

And though I ſpeake it with a penſiue heart,

Yet let me adde to this a ſecond part.

When that ſame vnion which the bodie ties

Vnto the ſoule, diſſolued is, and dies;

When that the one doth from the other goe,

After the farewell, workes the fleſh or noe?

Tis cleare it doth not. We may then inferre,

Since it doth neither ſee, ſpeake, moue, or
    ſtirre,

The ſpirit doth viuificate, and make

The bodie fit to act, and vndertake.

Shee, ſhee alone giues motion to each part,

The eies, the tongue, the armes, the feete,
    the heart.

Tis onely ſhee, that doth a beeing giue

To wretched man, that doth not breath, nor
    liue,

                P p   But

But by her functions: if shee flie away,
The bodie a dull carcasse doth decay;
And turnes to putrefaction, dust, and earth,
The proper substance, whence it hath its birth.
Say that the flesh the will, the sense command,
Admit that passion in defiance stand:
Yet in the act they alwayes do fall short,
Vnlesse the vital spirit do support;
This from the soule his operation takes,
Which dies vnacted, when her vigour slackes.
The dead sinne not, although the liuing do,
Tis yet when as the soule concurres thereto:
Take off her working, what remaines to sense?
A dull dead being, free from all offence.
How then with so great confidence can shee
Make the flesh guiltie, yet her selfe be free?
The murther'd man is with a dagger kill'd,
The hand offends, for it the dagger held:
Incensed passion did the hand prouoke,
Spirit gaue strength, and strength the fatal
          stroke:
The harmelesse weapon in it selfe is freed,
The hand's then guiltie, that perform'd the
          deed:
Passion acquites the hand, the fault was hers,
But shee the cause vnto the soule transfers;
Since that from her the actiue power flew,
That heart and hand vnto the motion drew.
                                        Poyson

Poyson the life of some one man confounds,
He makes it fatal , that the drugge com-
    pounds,
The venom hurts not, if it do not finde
Giuers and takers for the plot assig'nde.

Sense may discerne , but cannot iudge of
    things,
Tis reason that the resolution brings:
Reason doth from the soule immortal grow,
Whose onely power doth make it see and
    know:
So that in all we do by reason act,
It is the soule, that must auow the fact.
Tis shee alone, and none but shee doth make
The bodie see, know, choose, and vndertake.
Powder subuerts, and blowes vp all that stands
Within its compasse, nothing countermands
Its furie : yet in its owne proper course
It hurts not: till the fier doth giue force,
When raging vpward it in thunder flies,
Till in the act its force and furie dies:
Our passions so, that are the subiects fit
To flame on each occasion, and commit
A violence vpon those vertues, which
The mind direct, enlighten, and enrich:
Breake neuer into action, till they be
Fir'd with those sparkles, from the soule that
    flee :

There dwells the substance, which the lightnig
    flings,
Which kindling, soone a sad destruction brings,
Shee may in iustice then at least confesse,
Shee is as guiltie, as the sinnefull flesh.
Besides her contradictiue power, shee might
By her directions still haue kept me right.
O Spirit, Spirit, hadst thou beene aduis'd,
And thy Creators loue but truly pris'd:
Hadst thou lou'd God, whiles we were heere
    aliue,
Being dead, we should with glorie yet reuiue.
Vnto the poore that did assistance craue
Hadst thou beene kinde, it had adorn'd my
    graue:
Sighes, teares, and prayers from the heart
    exprest
Had crown'd our end, and future being blest.
Nor time, nor death, nor change had from vs
    snatcht
Our honours, with our goodnes sweetlie
    matcht.
Nor thou, nor I had thus complaining stood,
Rankt in the number of that cursed broode.
But now behold the sad remaines of all,
Earth doth contemne, and heau'n abhorre
    our fall.
Wormes, putrefaction, and a loathed bead

                  Are

Are the reward at best, now we are dead.
Nay (which is worser farre) we must appeare
Among the damned at that Audict, where
That fatal sentence will be so exprest,
That we thence forth can neuer hope for rest:
But must in euerlasting torments dwell,
A prey for those vnsatiat iawes of hell.
Heere from the depth of a deiected hart,
Which to too late his sorrow doth impart,
Forth by the organs of his hollow voyce
Breakes out a murmuring, sad, confused noyse,
With sighes and grones, that ecchoed horrid
    feare :
The flesh doth pause, and its complaints for-
    beare.
In height of passion it a respit takes,
Whiles the tormeted soule this answere makes.

The Soule.

ACcursed Flesh, whose impudence pre-
    sumes
By an vsurped power, which thou resumes
Vniustlie, thus to taxe thy soueraignes deedes,
Whose dearest partes by thy rebellion bleedes.
Know, all thy glosing rhetorick is too weake,
Although thou couldst in more perfection
    speake,

Tt

To take off from thy selfe thy proper guilt;
Which hath these ruins thus defac'd, and spilt.
It is in vaine to intimate or show,
Those foule disorders in thy bosome grow:
Since with a brasen face thou durst denie,
That which is seene by each indifferent eie.
But thou hast yet those straines of flesh and
    blood,
Which iustifies it selfe, and will make good
The foulest errors with a bloodlesse cheeke,
If a dead palsie do the conscience strike.
This is a Maxime, that such monsters, flie
To dare to doe, and yet not dare denie.
I will no more thus spend my wearie breath,
Vnto the eare that is to dull, or deafe:
Let me in freedome onely thus much say,
Twas thy foule treason cast vs both away.
Oh, had I trulie knowne the state of things,
I then had shunn'd the cause this terrour
    brings.
Might I retread the iournrey which I went,
I would auoid the feare, the paines preuent:
But hopes and wishes now are fruitlesse, vaine:
Nor wordes, nor teares, nor time can free-
    dome gaine.
Why was I borne, why did I breath, or liue,
If this be the reward the end doth giue?
Why did great God my birth or life permit,
                 When

When he forknew I muſt be damn'd by it?
Was his Sonnes ſuffering mankind might be
    free,
That died for all, and yet not died for me?
Curſt be the minute gaue my being breath,
Curſt be the life reſign'd it ſelfe to death.
Curſt be the ſtock, of which I was compos'd,
Curſt be the wombe, that me at firſt diſclos'd.
Curſed be all, that did concurre to frame
This curſed piece of ſorrow, ſinne, and shame.
Is this the goodnes and the mercie great,
Of which ſo many tõgues, and volumes treate,
To caſt in rigour a poore ſoule away,
That being ſeduced and betrayd did ſtray?
A ſoule of his owne making, which did weare
His glorious liuerie, and his image beare.
Fathers chaſtiſe, but none their children kill,
Although they be rebellious to their will.
The world's great Father is more cruel farre,
To thoſe which are his owne, that guiltie are.
Not for an hower, a day, a yeare, an age,
But he for euer doth poore man engage
Into the depth of torment, where exil'd,
Obdurate he, will n'ere be reconcil'd.
No crueltie on earth was euer ſuch,
But at the laſt would ſome compaſſion touch.
The beaſt is happie, he in this is bleſt,
In that his ſpirit with his fleſh deceaſt,

                                The

They both together to deſtruction goe,
And no ſuch paines by after reckoning know.
Death is the worſt, and all that he need feare,
Which brings perpetual reſt, quite void of care.
The flow'r, whome weeping April doth beget,
In her faire veſture to the view is ſet:
It buddes and bloſſomes, pleaſing to the eie,
And doth enioy its ſeaſon, and then die:
Although with ſenſe of ioy it doth not grow,
Dead or aliue, it doth no ſorrow know.
Vn happie man, vnto the world appeares
A wretched thing, that hath nought els but
        teares:
His mothers torment, and his fathers care,
Shame to himſelfe, ſo faint, ſo weake, ſo bare:
His mind and bodie ſcarce a minute free,
To diſcontent and ſicknes wedded be.
His pilgrimage in ſad affliction goes,
Wandring throughout a wildernes of woes:
Clogg'd with the luggage which his caſſock
        hides,
That he in vaine for his returne prouides.
In cragged wayes, through deſerts vncooth,
        fill'd
With murthering theeues, that paſſengers haue
        kill'd.
He iogges along in feare, ſcarce taking reſt,
Whiles he with ſtormes, and tepeſts is oppreſt.
                                        The

The glorious sunne-shinne toles along his
    sense,
The golden vallies do some ioy commence.
When sodainely black night and furious
    clowdes
    Within whose bosomes fatal mischiefe
    shrowdes
Her venome spleene) do ouertake him so,
He can by no meanes one step further goe.
The out-law death, vnarm'd doth him sur-
    prise,
And like a tyrant kills him, thus he dies.
Dead to the world, the debt of nature paid,
He findes himselfe in deeper bandes betraid:
Which are not cacelld, till the score be clear'd,
Though this engagement he hath scarcely
    fear'd.
What then ensues? He must in bondage lie,
Dying with torments, yet must neuer die.
Thus do the greater plagues but then beginne,
When the first warrefare endes in shame and
    sinne.
But peace, no more; no more, thou canst not
    ease
(As sick men do) discoursing thy disease.
Fond Flesh be gone, and haste thee to thy
    vrne :
As I must now, thou shalt in torments burne.

            Qq   Till

Till then goe feed the hungrie wormes , and
    graue :
I must obey, that am great Plutoes Slaue.

The Bodie.

THe Bodie, which with sad attention heard
    This dull relation, was much more affeard.
The foule is now beleeu'd, whome liuing, hee
Had slighted so, that they could scarce agree.
The first propensions Nature did infuse ,
Makes him euen now, inquisitiue of newes,
Wooing the Soule, being scortcht with raging
    heat,
For some progression, ere shee did retreat:
Which for a parting, and a last farewell,
Might intimate the passages of hell.
To which effect he soulders vp the breach,
And with a milder current makes his speach.
Thou which wert once my guest (poore gro-
    ning Ghost)
If thow hast seiourn'd in that neather coast,
I pray thee tell me, what thou there hast seene,
What hath thy chance or entertainement
    beene.
What priuiledge, or more promotion there,
Do nobler persons find, or riches share?
Will the tormentors bribed bee, or fee'd,
                                That

That so by gold, or guifts they may be freede?
Can the prerogatiue of birth or grace,
Or strength of wit repriue vs from that place?
May they not vndermine, or by plaine force
Themselues from such a loathsome gaile di-
    uorce?
Cannot a quirk in law some errour find,
By which we may those cruel bondes vnbind?
Or be remoued by a write of right
From that black center of eternal night?
Are not the barres or locks to be vndoone,
May not the wardens there be wrought vpon?
If there be hopes of their redemption, tell,
Forth from the bowells of deuouring hell.
Me thinkes there cannot be a place secure,
That can for euer hold out, or endure.
Where gold, wit, strength, and craft do all
    combine,
To make the captiue be a libertine.
If that entreaties cannot there preuaile,
Prisonners yet find pittie in the gaile.
Speake what thou know'st, although it come
    to late,
Yet tis some ease, to know the worst of fate.

The

The Soule.

THy question (Flesh) is fond, and void of
    sense:
If thou beleeue the soules departed hence
All black and foule, polluted, deeplie died,
With scarlet sinnes, with sinnes vnpurified,
(Being confind to euerlasting paine)
Can be redeem'd, or ransom'd back againe.
All hope in hell is hopelesse , though it brings
The high command and priuiledge of Kings.
Entreaties there are fruitlesse , prayers lost,
Compassion neuer harbour'd in that coast.
No depth of pollicie can ouer reach ,
No humane strength, or wit can force a breach.
Vnited strengthes of Monarches are to
    weake,
One gate of hell to open , force, or breake.
Bribes be reiected, though the bribers be
Of this black corporation all made free.
Beautie, proportion, shape ; though louely
    heere,
Find intertainement there , but sorrie cheere.
Almes, prayers, fasting, all those pious deedes,
Which the deuotion of the liuing feedes,
Cannot obtaine one sparke , or myte of grace,
For those sad soules , that do possesse this place.
                      Should

Should the whole world do nothing els but
    pray,
It cannot ease their torment one poore day.
If all the Church did nothing els but fast,
One drop of mercie these can neuer taste.
Stroue all that all, that all, the world can bring,
Or think, or hope, or wish; the furious sting
Of hell nor endes , nor lessens one poore
    dramme,
In time, in sense, in paine, in horrour, shame.
Hope hath no ground , nor reason to suppose
A hope of freedome from so cruel foes.
Into whose cruel hands if once we fall,
Nor heau'n , nor earth, nor they will heare
    our call.
Know that the man, on earth that hath possest
The quintessence of all, we count the best
Of worldly blessings : findes in hell no more
Respect or comfort (though he do implore
That did command) then doth the poorest
    groome,
Which in this cursed place hath a sad roome.
Although he had command by land and sea,
His iurisdiction heere can hold no plea.
He cannot that great parliament our-face,
Nor those same pillars of the state disgrace:
Nor can he crush the poorest vassaile heere,
Or make the greater stoope, or yeeld for feare.

                       He

He can haue heere no gard, no porters fet,
To keepe the fuburbes of his cabinet:
Yet he shall be attended, but with those,
Shall load him euerie minute with their
    blowes.
And let him know, his former greatnes shall
Not fink an ace, although the maifter fall.
More then he kept before to ferue his pride,
He shall haue heere, to pinch and lace his fide.
Nor can he be fet free, or make retreat,
If all the kingdome fue, and king entreat.
The proud infulting diuel will not giue
The meaneft foule that in his gyues doth liue:
Though in exchange he might haue millions
    heere,
Nor fuffer, that it do not fuffer there.
But where thou feekeft to know what is pre-
    par'd
For those fame glorious monfters, that haue
    shar'd
The marrow of the earth, and fcrude it thence,
By all those wayes, that might delight the
    fenfe.
Know, thefe great turretts in their ruines
    winne
In equal meafure torments to their finne.
Great Lucifer doth not with one difpence,
Or giue diftinction, or preheminence

                   In

In point of priuiledge; although in paine
Some more, some lesse (as they deseru'd) do
   gaine.

The wealthy miser newlie dead and damn'd,
Hath his vnsatiat iawes heere fully cramm'd.

The Statist with his Atheisme, there can
   tell,
There is an heau'n, but he hath found a hell.

The vniust Iudge, that iustlie is condemn'd,
Findes heere his person scorn'd, his powre
   contemn'd.

The drunkard in his vomit heere hath found
Roome to corouse, where liquor doth abound.

Luxurious lust, that neuer conscience made,
Findes heere shee-diuells store of his owne
   trade.

The murtherer that did delight in blood,
Findes heere an Ocean, and may drinke a
   flood.

The proudest Sire, may heere finde spirits
   store,
As proud as he, and if not ten-times more.

The hypocrite, that his religion makes,
Feeles what they suffer, that the Church for-
   sakes.

The Fauourite, whose crymsen sinnes in
   graine
Are matchlesse: such his horrour and his paine,
                  Though

Though he on earth could flatter, fawne, and
　creepe,
A Ganimede great Pluto will not keepe.
Vnlesse he be in scalding liquor boild,
Or drest in scortching flames, and freelie oyl'd.
Nor can the greatest King or Monarch sway,
There he must suffer all, and all obey.
His royall ornaments are all defac'd,
His titles lost, and crowne; himselfe disgrac'd
Must suffer for his proper sinnes, and those,
They haue committed, whome his dotage
　chose.
Yet are his tormehts matcht and fitted so,
That they his sinne, and his condition show.
The punishments in heil are thus transferr'd,
In kind, and full proportion as they err'd.
Alone this difference pens or tongues may
　speake
Their faultes and sinnes: yet these are both to
　weake,
To shew their torments, which are greater
　farre,
Then all the power of man's expressions are.
Which I so trulie feele, my heart growes dull:
Flesh now adieu, for I haue spoke at full.

　　　　　　　　　　　　　　　　The

The Author.

VVIth this (me thought) a hurling tempest blew,
Which did not wake me, but my dreame renew.
Midnight the patronesse of wandring Sprites,
And walking ghosts (whose apparition frightes
The amaz'd beholder) newlie had begunne
To call vp Hesper, to goe meete the sunne:
Whose fierie chariot made such thúdring haste,
That he the neather world had almost past.
The mornings watchman from his warbling
        throat,
Gaue his first summons in a hollow noate.
The howling dogges and scritch fowles seem'd
        to tell,
A pursuiuant was come with newes from hell.
Forthwith me thought, I saw two fiendes ap-
        peare,
Blacker then blackest pitch or night they
        were.
No pen or pencill of the choicest art
Can character their shapes in euerie part.
So horrid, ghastlie, pale, so meagre, leane,
So fierce, so cruel, rugged, so vncleane.
Their grimme aspects, and dogged lookes
        were such,

            R r   That

That I did feare to fee, but loath'd to touch.

A shiuering faintnes (herbinger of feare)

Tainted my fpirits, feiz'd me euerie where.

My blood his pipes and channells all for-
        fooke,

And fwiftlie to my heart his iourney tooke:

Which hearing this Allarum ftoodlie ftood

His ftation: and refolu'd to make it good,

Being vndaunted: bidding me attend

Each paffage well, and to obferue the end.

After fome few harsh-hollow-fouding noates,

Which grombling came in thunder from their
        throates,

Like to the roaring of a Lioneffe,

When shee hath found fome beaft in fuch di-
        ftreffe,

That he cannot auoid her angrie pawes.

Sends forth a murmure from her hungrie
        iawes,

Which ecchoing from the woodes vnto the
        plaines,

Frightes both the flocks, and all the shepheard
        fwaines:

Such was the noife thefe curfed hell-houndes
        made,

When they in furie this poore foule inuade.

They brandish gads of fteele red hoat, and
        caft

Great

Great flames of brimstoue, which they did
  exhauft
Forth from their yawning mouthes, whofe
  portalls kept
A double gard of fangs, in venome fteept;
That fnarling ground themfelues, and feem'd
  to feed
Vpon the flauering foame, that did proceed
Forth from the furnaces of furie, where
Dwelt nought but mifchiefe, and iuft caufe of
  feare.
Their glarie eies all fierie, great, and fierce,
Flafhes of lightning (as they roule) difperfe:
Squinting their glaunces with fuch peerfing
  beames,
That the whole roome feem'd full of fierie
  ftreames.
About their necks huge curled' fnakes hung
  downe,
Hiffing in knottie clufters, venome throwne
From their black forked tongues, which
  quiuering fhake,
As if they all had beene but one great fnake.
Forth from their fnoaring noftrills cloudes of
  fmoke
Came wreaking out, as they the world would
  choke,
Making a fullen darknes, which did fmell,

Worfer then any ftench, faue that of hell.

Their lowling eares had iffues, whence did
flow

Streames of corruption : on their forc-heads
grow

Brow antlers sharpe, in liquid poyfon dípt;

Their nailes (like wilde boares tuskes) their
fingers tipt.

Bodies like toades, with their owne venome
fwell'd,

And bellies great, with flaming fulpher fill'd.

Armes all imblifterd o're with boyles and
blaines,

With clouen feete, and legges that mow'ed in
chaines.

Thefe tooke the foule, and hal'd her vnder
ground,

In boiftrous cordage, and in fetters bound.

Whofe bitter moanes, and fad lamenting cries

Did ecchoing feeme to pearfe and teare the
skies.

To bid her well-come crowdes of fpirits
flocke,

With yelling howles, that her deride and
mocke:

Like apes they friskoll, and their anticks play,

As if in hell it had beene holie day.

And certainely if in that darkfome caue

The

The damned any mirth, or solace haue,
They did reioyce to welcome such a guest,
As by their gestures seem'd to be exprest.
When they their staring eies had glutted soe,
Like rauening wolues they do their furie shew,
Gnashing their teeth ; each one his parte
    beginns,
With towest thongs some twinge her flesh,
    that spinns
With wreaking blood : some powre on molten
    lead,
Some teare her downe with ir'n-hookes fierie
    red.
Some spout foule vrine in her smarting eies,
Some fetch her food forth from their filthie
    sties.
Some cram'd her ioynts, vntill her sinowes
    crackt,
Whiles others crusht her lymmes, and bodie
    rackt:
Some did annoint her or'e with scalding oyle,
Which blistering vp did so her beautie spoile;
That all her skinne and whitenes thus trans-
    form'd,
Seem'd like a leaper, whiles their Maistres
    burn'd.
All with their teeth did teare and grinde her
    soe,

                      That

That shee did seeme quite flead, from top to
    toe.

In this hard plight and suffering; fearefull cries

Flew through her eares, whiles her sad wee-
    ping eies

On either side beholdes whole legions stand

Of ouglie mishap monsters, scortcht and tand,

With the reflection of those fierie beames,

Which did enlighten the darke caue with
    streames,

That sparkling flew, whiles all the fiends did
    roare

In thunder, as if they hell gates had toare.

The Diuells.

TYr'de at the length, these ouglie hell-
    hounds crie,

See heere the place, whore thou shalt euer lie.

We honour thus our friends : now heau'n
    implore,

Or hell coniure: It will auaile no more.

Thou art our owne, we now haue made thee
    sure,

Heere thou must suffer these, and more en-
    dure.

No time out runnes thy torment heere fast
    tied,

                      Thou

Thou muſt be plagu'd with paines ſtill cen-
    tuplide.

Thou hadſt all worldlie pleaſure, ſpents thy
    time,

Of all the ioyes on earth thou hadſt the prime.

Who durſt oppoſe thine actions, or conteſt,

But felt thy raging furie, and did reſt

On termes of certaine danger, which did wait

Thy endes, with open force, or cloſe deceit?

Such was thy vertue howſoe're thou ſmilde,

Where thou didſt hate, thou ne're wert re-
    concilde.

We fed thy humour, ſooth'd, and did aſſiſt,

At no one turne we thy aduantage miſt.

Didſt thou beleeue we ſeru'd thee for meere
    loue,

Which neuer yet could make a diuel moue?

No; twas to gaine thee as a lawfull prize,

We did our engins lay, and plots deuize.

No reaſon then we ſhould haue beene debard

Of that we long'd for, thee our iuſt reward.

If thou didſt liuing feare, or hate vs, why

Didſt thou then vs, vnto thy ſeruice tie?

Thou foundſt the craſie world to looke a ſquint

On vertuous goodnes, though it came in print.

And from this ground by ſtrong ambition led,

With looſe deſires was thy corruption fed.

To ſecond thine intentiõs (this way bent)

                  Thou

Thou foughoſt and gain'ſt full quicklie our
    aſſent,
To make thee great : which greatnes caught
    thee ſo,
That in ſhort time thy ſelfe thou didſt not
    know :
But (as we hop'd) didſt proue ſo looſe, ſo proud,
That earth contemn'd, what heauen diſauow'd.
Perhaps thou thoughtſt, and didſt beleeue, that
    we
Might when and how thou pleaſedſt, cooz'ned
    be.
So ſeeled doues do towring blindfold flie,
Hoping to get protection from the skie :
Vntill the mounting haggard haue out-flowne
The ſo ill-guided haſte her wings haue ſhowne.
Seiz'd as a prey, ſhee ſtoopes downe to the
    ground,
Taxing her pride, that hath ſuch danger found.
Alas, in vaine thou didſt thy hopes repoſe
Vpon ſo faint aſſurances as thoſe ;
Which make a fluttering ſhew, as if that they,
Could flie vp ſtraight to heau'n, and knew the
    way.
Their hood-winckt zeale, that do that doctrine
    preach,
Forſake their mother Church, and fancies
    teach:

                                        (Fancies

(Fancies that are their owne, which best agree
With those, on earth that hunt for libertie)
We do commend, aud foreward what we can
The pur-blind wayes, and errours of that man,
Which to himselfe doth his religion make,
And doth the long continued truth forsake.
Such make the place so full wherein we dwell,
And do improue the Monarchie of hell.
But thou I thinke couldst force the leasure
    finde,
To let religion so possesse thy mind.
But for a minute, that thou mightst haue tr ,
The gold from drosse, and it haue purifide, ♦
It was enough (as thou beleeu'dst) to winne,
A death-bed vantage, to repent thy sinne.
Forestall'd in this, lo where thy fortune lies,
Thy bodie dead, thy torment neuer dies.
Seest thou thy well-come, is it good and
    faire?
This entertainement neuer shall empaire.
Though thou aliue hadst friends and seruants
    store,
Yet heere be sure, thou shalt haue ten times
    more:
That at an inch will waite vpon thee so,
Thou shalt no want of thy prouision know.
Our grimme great Maister, whome on earth
    thou serud'st

          will

Will pay the wages, thou to well deferud'ft.
Thy penfion ne're shall ceafe, wee'l fee it payd,
In full aboundance, be not then difmaid.
With this afresh they do renue their blowes,
Tearing the wretched foule, halfe dead with
woes.

Th' Soule.

VVIth deepe heart-breaking fighes, and
saddeft cries
that from the bitternes of forrow flies,
With teares and grones, a fad lamenting noife
The foule, thus vs'd, doth eleuate her voyce,
Screeking and fcreaming, hopeleffe, full of
paine,
Which in each part did in full height remaine.
Such were her lamentations, fuch her moanes,
They were fent back from riuers, woodes,
and ftones:
By their shrill ecchoes, which reiterate,
As if they did her griefe participate.
Shee ftrugling striu'd to cleare, and fo fet
free
Her felfe entangled, from their tyrannie.
But (ah, alas) her ftrength was to too weake
To make it good, that had fcarce powre to
fpeake.

As

As well as her distracted wordes could wooe,
Shee humbly begges, that they would let her
    goe.
The hardest heart had melted to behold
Her drooping teares, which her condition told.
As when a heard of rauenous woulfes haue
    found
Some goodly weather , prostrate on the
    ground;
Straid from the shepheard, and the flock he
    led
With his dull sounding bell, vnto their feed;
They set vpon him with their furious pawes ,
And teare his skinne with their deuouring
    iawes:
Whiles he a prisoner to their malice, striues,
But all in vaine; his strugling nought contriues,
May win his freedome, or procure his peace;
The more he straines, the more his woes en-
    creafe;
Till at the last his trickling teares assay,
To gaine his pardon by some milder way:
Which sadlie bleating out submissiue woes
Entreates for pittie, where no pittie growes.
Hopelesse at length, despairing he lies still,
Suffering his cruel foes to worke their will:
So fares it with this wretched soule distrest
(The bell weather, that in his life possest

Ss 2   Vnder

Vnder the shepheard, in the flock chiefe place
For high promotion, honour, wealth, and grace)
Seizd by these curst tormentors, which had
　　catcht
Her at the vantage they long time had watcht.
They vent their malice, whiles shee seekes to
　　free
Her selfe from such a base captiuitie.
Finding the vigour of her proper strength
Too faint and feeble; shee resolues at length
To trie if her entreaties might preuaile,
To set her loose from such a loathsome gayle:
But when shee found their hearts (as heard
　　as steele)
Did no one touch of true compassion feele,
But that her liquid teares fell fruitlesse
　　downe,
Answered with scorne : as one quite ouer-
　　throwne,
Shee fainting yeeldes, and with her hollow
　　cries
Makes hell the witnes of her miseries.
Crying (when shee grimme Plutoes threshold
　　trod)
I E S V, the Sonne of Dauid, Sonne of God.

The

The Diuells.

TH'enraged fiendes at this began to shake,
Their hearts at that great name did trem-
bling quake:
Their roaring bellowes stopt her mournefull
crie,
While in derision they do thus replie.
Too late, too late thou now in vaine dost striue
Or seeke diuine assistance: this aliue
Might haue redeemed thee: it is now too
late
The worldes Redeemers name to inuocate.
A *Miserere* cannot helpe thee heere;
Nor helpe, nor hope of pardon can appeare.
Sit still, and suffer: this must be thy way,
Curse, and blaspheme, tis fitter then to pray.
Thou seest thou art an Outcast, quite bereaft
Of heau'n, and hast no hope of comfort leaft.
To what end then shouldst thou his aid im-
plore,
That hauing bought thee, made of thee no
store?
Thou seest the glorie of thy morning bright
Is turn'd to darknes, and eternal night.
The luster of thine eie; dull, dead, and
chang'd,

Thy

Thy fresh faire cheekes now pale, and quite
    estrang'd.
The beautie of thy face, and bodie spoild,
Thy mind with horrour more and more
    embroyld.
No minute free, no part exempt, no age
Thy torment can take off, or griefe aswage.
What then remaines but euerlasting shame,
To make thee hate thy being, curse thy name?
But hearke, the hollow windes begin to rise,
The prince of darknes calls to sacrifice.
We must be gone vnto the lower deepe ,
Where Elphins, Fairies, and Hobgoblins keepe
The fatal Audict, how they haue discharg'd
Their seueral duties, how they haue enlarg'd
Hells Monarchie. All now their tribute bring,
And prostrate, lay it downe before the King.
Within our regiment we thee enroule
From this time forth ; be this thy comfort ,
    Soule.

The Author.

THe tragick Epilogue did thus conclude,
    That did my dreaming fancie thus delude.
The sad appearance was so liuely showne,
My dreaming fancie made it waking knowne.
The deepe impressions of so strange a sight
           Startled

Startled mine eies, and did my sleepe affright.
All in a trembling feare amaz'd, I wake,
Yet could not this *Fantasma* from me shake,
Me thought his passage intimated more,
Then I had dream'd, or euer seene before.
Which call'd me vp, and made me leaue my
    bed,
And to deuotion my amazement led.
When I awhile had sifted, and suruaid,
And to my iudgement had the sense conuaid
Of what I seem'd to heare, behold, and see,
I did conclude, it should an instance be,
To teach me how to innouate my wayes,
And mould anew my former mispent dayes.
Which with more speed and care for to effect
I straight wayes did my hands and heart erect,
And on my bended knees did there entreat
Diuine protection from those paines so great.
Framing my meditations to attend
Those ioyes that blesse the graue, and crowne
    the end.
Hence forth fond world adieu, I thee despise,
And from thy witchcraft will withdraw mine
    eies :
Mine eies, that too too lõg haue wãdring gone,
And left the marke vnseene, vnthought vpon:
The blessed marke, for which they were or-
    dain'd,

            which

Which by repentant teares is onely gain'd.
Giue honour, iewells, high promotion, wealth,
Reuenues, pleasures, foueraigntie, and health,
Alas what are they? Tranfitorie things,
Which carelesse foules vnto destruction brings.
If we abufe them, on the reckoning day
For our contempt we too too dearely pay.
If they be bleffings, they be onely lent,
Whiles we within this cage of life are pent.
They goe not with vs, when we fleepe in
      death,
Nor can they giue the lungs, of life one breath.
He that doth want them all, liues yet content,
Well pleas'd with what the God of peace hath
      fent.
He that enioyes them for a feafon heere,
Goes heauie laden, doubtfull, full of feare.
Yet thefe inchant the willing mind to winne,
A minutes pleafure for a world of finne.
The ftragling eie, is quicklie led aftray,
And shadowes do the willing heart betray.
Inueigling thus the Maiftreffe of the mind,
That is to nobler aymes and workes affign'd:
Vntill at laft pale death doth fo preuent,
They haue no time to mend, or to repent.
What followes then? My pen abhorres to tell:
Let them recite, that driue a trade with hell.
No more, no more will I on thefe attend,

                              But

But vnto God my selfe, and thoughtes com-
    mend.
Looke on the world (but with vnpartiall eies)
Things change their liueries, Fooles do foole
    the wise.
Deuotion doth grow cold, truth's banisht
    hence,
Man doth not rule by reason, but by sense.
Iustice is famisht, where Religion failes,
Tumultuous faction in the state preuailes.
Who feares to act, when he may freely keepe
His owne transgressions vnconfest, asleepe?
Who makes a conscience to doe that is ill,
When conscience is become but great men's
    will?
Alas the world to ruine runnes amaine,
Men do adore the golden Calfe againe.
He that on earth is rich and glorious, thriues,
Held as a God, his worship now surviues.
He shall be sooth'd, and pleas'd, although he be
A peece compos'd of perfect treacherie.
The man whose fortunes be decaid and poore,
Sittes on the threshold, enters not the dore.
If that his vertue be both good and great,
It scarce will winne him credit, cloathes, and
    meat.
Like to a garment rich and costlie made,
Whose outside doth his inward goodnes shade

If that the fashion change, or nap be worne,
It is laid by, and with a kind of scorne
Sequestred from the wardrope, which doth
  hold
No robes, but those, whose outside daub'd with
  gold
Doth fit the time, and garbe; although they be
For vse or warmth much short in each degree:
So fares it with sincere and vertuous truth,
Which cannot pleate the straines of vitious
  youth.
It is enough, that shee is old, and fits,
No giddie humor of Fantastick wits.
Shee is not thread-bare but is better linde,
Then those new Antick shapes, which seeme
  refinde
Shee is more comely, wholesome, more secure,
And doth a tenne-times longer time endure.
These cannot yet her credit so preserue,
That shee may please the time, or maister serue:
But with a too vnworthy scornefull doome
Shee is cast by into some vncouth roome:
Where vnrespected, shee in darknes dwells,
Supported by her innocence, nought els.
Such is the entertainemeut Vertue findes
In these foule, canckred, and corrupted
  mindes.
Diuine Theologie is almost dead,

                              And

And those her vertuous daughters gone and
    fled.

Faith Hope, and Charitie, that ware the
    wreath

Of honour lately, now do scarcely breath.

No wonder, where false Heresie doth lurch,

To robbe the Sainctes, and to subuert the
    Church.

Deceipt and auarice do as they pleafe

Rule, and vndoe vaine men with flights, at
    eafe.

Ambition that sweet Syren still doth call

Our aymes vp high, to catch the greater fall.

None by defert do rife, tis onely fate,

And impudence, that do aduance the state.

Canft thou deriue thy pedigree, and show

The blood is noble, in thy vaines doth flow.

Art thou well qualified, with iudgement, wit,

With vertuous goodnes, for employment fit,

Haft thou a modest tongue, a heart fincere,

A hand vnstained, and an infide cleare.

Canft thou be courteous, humble, full of truth,

Enioyft thou valor, vigour, strength & youth.

Nay (which is more) haft thou Religion kept,

And with a guiltlesse conscience sweetly slept:

All these are yet no motiues to aduance,

Where Money leades the measure, footes the
    dance.

        If

If thou haſt her, thoſe other titles ſlow,
As if they did withi in thy marrow giow.
What can he want, that is poſſeſt of gold,
Where all things are for Money bought and
    ſold?
Honour aduancement, iuſtice, places high,
Are ſet at ſale, to him will deareſt buy.
The verie charge of ſoules doth riſe and fall,
The fatteſt purſe the market doth fore-ſtall.
Nothing doth ſcape vncheapned, and vn-
    bought,
That hath or profit, or a title brought.
Vertue alone (the ſubiect of their hate)
Sittes like a turtle, that hath loſt her mate.
Perchance if thou canſt flatter, thou maiſt
    thriue,
Since honeſt truth againſt the ſtreame doth
    ſtriue.
Yet if thy tongue be oyld to make thee riſe,
Thou ſhalt ſtick faſt, vnleſſe thou temporize.
Be ſure to ſing the tune thy Patrone ſings,
Although it be againſt the King of kings:
And then thou maiſt be thought an Agent fit,
To haue a place in Councel for thy wit.
Then if thou canſt diſpoſe things wiſely ſoe,
That with the ſtreame thou canſt both ebbe and
    flow.
Match but thy ſelfe vnto ſome femal peece,

                                    That

That is Seianus cosin, Aunt, or neece,
Feare not , sheele quickly make thee higher
farre ,
Then those great Grandies , which more
antient are.

It is an age, that gently smiles on those,
That rather will their soules, then profit lose.
A great mans pandor (as the case now standes)
By his employment getts both wealth and
landes.

A spie, that swift intelligence can giue,
Cannot want meanes in such a way to liue.
But he that slily, can insinuate
Himselfe into the depth of men of state,
Acting their plotts with secrecie and skill;
Be it to vndermine, roote vp , or kill
Those, that do shade their endes,
which like the Eagle mounting still ascendes;
This man must rise, and it is reason good,
He buyes promocion with the price of blood :
Selling his soule to gaine and purchase hell,
No wonder, if on earth he prosper well.

In that same plaine and vertuous fore-right
way,
True worth and merit euer loose the day :
Their owners (honest fooles) are farre vnfit
To act in state where men must rise by wit.
There is no hope (beleeue it) to get vp,

Where

Where cunning drawes, and falshood fills the
    cup :
Vnlesse thou wilt surrender vp and yield
Thy soule and conscience : so thou gainst the
    field.
We see the greater Peeres, that can maintaine
A faire proportion, and a courtlie traine,
Matcht in the tribe of greatnes, grounded men
By natiue birth-right, yet if honest , then
They lessen by degrees, whiles vpstarts rise
Into their roomes, and them (cast downe)
    despise.
We see a solid worth, vpright, and iust,
That in his proper verrue puts his trust,
Scorn'd, and contemn'd, and geered to his
    face,
Whiles some poore puchsist doth possesse his
    place.
If we looke further, we may there behold
Iudgement and iustice meerely bought and
    sold.
The poore man's cause must perish by his
    want,
Money or fauour doth his right supplant;
Although he gaine a verdit he may leese,
Double the vantage in the lawyers fees:
Whose griping height is growne to such a rate,
A cause or two blowes vp a man of state.

                                    Yet

Yet for all this the world we court and hugge,
In which with restlesse care we striue & tugge.
O Vanitie of loue, conceptions poore,
Indulgent dotage, which doth barre the dore
To those celestial ioyes, which crowned be
With fulnes, and with blest eternitie.
Why doth man value so his griefe and shame,
Pleasures, that wast more swift then flaxe in
    flame.
Since he enioyes them, and doth onely share
Delightes by minutes , cloggd with monthes
    of care?
The glimmering sunne in sullé winter showes
His sparkling beames awhile, and straitway
    goes
Into some cloud, that doth congealed lie,
Wrapt vp in foldes, within the azure skie:
Which melting sendes downe showers of raine
    and hayle,
Whose teares vpon her beautie cast a vaile:
Then follow furious tempests , thunder,
    winde,
The earth growes darke, and all the welkin
    blinde.
So that the rising sunne-shine rests obscure,
And doth whole dayes of mourning sad en-
    dure.
Nor is it wonder, when one onely sunne

              Tho-

Thorough an armie of black cloudes muſt
　　runne.
And in the brighteſt ſplendor of his rayes,
Be ſet vpon, ſo many ſeueral wayes.
Our winters ioy a little warmth may taſte,
But it out-runnes it ſelfe, and makes ſuch
　　haſte,
That it encounters an eclyps, which hides
His beames, that in ſo ſmall a circle bides.
Then ſtormes of care, and ſtrong afflictions
　　keepe
His glorie buried in a clowdie ſleepe.
Say that we haue a day that's faire and cleare,
That day each minute hath iuſt cauſe of feare.
Contentment (like the Phænix) flies alone:
Cares come in flocks, as crowes that are high
　　flowne.
Our ioyes are ſpū ſo fine, vnſtrain'd they crack,
Whiles ſorrow, like a cable, holdes vs rack.
No man aliue, that calenders his dayes,
But findes his griefe, his pleaſure faire o're-
　　ſwayes.
Yet we deſire to liue, are loath to die,
But to encreaſe our ſhame and miſerie.
Old age, (alas) doth but aduantage winne,
To ſuffer more, and to encreaſe our ſinne.
Who ſo betimes vnto his burial goes,
Goes lighter laden, and leſſe ſorrow knowes.
　　　　　　　　　　The

The world is as a wildernes o'regrowne,
Where paſſengers are loſt, and ouerthrowne.
He that doth in his iourney ſcape the beſt,
With thornes and brambles is each ſtep op-
　　preſt.
The way that leades to the Elyſian fieldes,
Is ruffe and rugged, which ſmall pleaſure
　　yieldes.
Vnto the Stygian lake the way is broad,
And hath an open, plaine, and eaſie road :
Which is the cauſe poore man, that wants a
　　guide;
Doth poſting on to his deſtruction ride.
Is this the ſumme of what we heere enioy,
The vintage vpon which we do employ
The vantage of the ſeaſon, and our ſtrength,
For want of fruit to be cut downe at length,
And caſt into the euer-burning flame,
As fuel fit for euerlaſting ſhame ?
Vnhappie man, that doſt purſue and ſtriue
To winne the world, in which thou canſt not
　　thriue.
With much more reaſon it might iuſtlie moue,
If this Impoſture, whome we ſo much loue,
Vnto the great ones theſe three things could
　　giue :
A luſtie youth continu'd; ſtill to liue :
And with a freſh encreaſe to gather more,

　　　　　　　　V u　　　　　　They

They might improue their ſtock, augment
    their ſtore,
Without an after reckoning, which ſuruayes
The former errours of the fore-paſt dayes.
But wretch, conſider how thy fortune ſtandes,
Death both thy life, and all thou haſt com-
    mandes.
Thy now faire cheekes, to morrow pale and
    wanne,
Thy beautie witherd, and thy vigor gone.
Decrepid age or ſicknes ſtops thy breath,
Or ſome miſchance procures a ſodaine death:
Whoſe all deuouring powre, commãding will,
Triumphant; man or firſt or laſt doth kill:
Who is aſſign'd to die, and yet not knowes
The place to which, being dead, he after goes.
Me thinke the thought of this should ſtrike
    each part
Of wretched man, and pearſe his wanton
    heart.
Making him quit the world betimes, and take
A more retired courſe, which doth forſake
Aſwell temptations, as the act of ſinne,
And thoſe ſame meanes, that do entice
    him in,
For to betray him in ſo ſweet a way,
Where ſenſe preuailing reaſon doth betray:
And yet at length this ſenſe doth trulie know,
                  And

And feele his falshood, that betraid' him soe.
Confider what thou art, and whether bound,
In reclus'd eares it cannot harshlie found.
Peruſe Death's letters patents, and then know,
That die thou muſt, and yet not when nor how.
Flie from the world, yeeld not to flesh and
    blood,
Let what thy tongue hath ſpoke, thy heart
    make good.
Let not the Ægyptian flesh-potts murmuring
    leade
Thee back into thoſe wayes, thou once didſt
    treade.
Although thy Verdict be from thee conceal'd,
Thus much thy bleſt Redeemer hath reueal'd:
They mercie find, that do for mercie pleade,
Where Angells, Sainctes, and Martyrs inter-
    ceade.

CER-

CERTAINE DEVOVT
Verſes, touching the vanitie of
the world.

WHy doth the world as ſlaue
 Liue vnder vaine glorie:
 Whoſe long'ſt proſperitie
 Is ſo tranſitorie?
So ſoone his powre and pompe
 Doth fade and paſſe away,
 As brickie potts, which are
 Compos'd and made of clay.
More credit maiſt thou giue
 To letters grau'd in ice:
 Then to the wily world
 That fadeth in a trice:
 Making great promiſes
 With ſhew of ſanctitie;
 Which yet are falſe, and void
 Of all true certaintie.
Rather giue eare to men,

which

Which do the truth relate;
Then to the wretched world's
Vaine, and vnconstant state;
Whose fancies are but fond,
And full of vanitie;
Whose studies and delights
Are void of veritie.
Tell me Where's Salomon,
    Whilome so gay and bright?
Where's Sampson now, that did
Surpasse in strength and might?
Where's fairest Absolon,
Whome all desir'd to see?
Or freindly Ionathas,
So full of courtesie?
Whether is Cæsar gone,
    That bore so great a sway?
Or the rich glutton, which
Sate eating al the day?
Tell me, where's Tully now
Famous for rhetoricke?
Or Aristoteles,
That had a wit so quicke?
So many noble men,
    Such ample space of times;
So many cleargie men,
So many stratagemes:
So many potent Kings,

                                    So

So great authoritie,
Are al now paſt and gone,
In twincling of an eie,
The glorie of this world
Is short, like to a feaſt;
And all the ioyes thereof,
Are but as one nights gueſt:
Which do withdraw man's heart
From heau'ns felicitie;
And leade him by the hand
To hellish miſerie.
O carcaſſe, meate for wormes!
O clot of earth and clay!
O night, ô vanitie,
That art ſo braue and gay:
not knowing, whether thou
Shalt till to morow liue;
Doe therefore good to all,
Whiles life will giue thee leaue.
This glorie of the flesh,
Which is ſo much eſteem'd;
Like to a flowre, or graſſe,
In holy Write is deem'd:
Or to a wither'd leafe,
Which with the winde is blowne;
For ſo this life of man
Is quickly ouerthrowne.
Nothing eſteeme as thine,

Which

which thou canst loose againe ;
That, which the world doth giue,
Seeke neuer to retaine :
Thinke on those heau'nly things,
That are aboue the skies;
THRICE BLESSED IS THAT MAN,
WHICH CAN THE WORLD DESPISE.

AN EXHORTATION
to penance, written in Latine by
D. Dominicke the
Carthusian.

Man, thou noble Creature, why
(Since thou knowst, that thou must
die)
Dost thou so much ouerprise
Fading pleasure, and despise
Those rich ioyes of Paradise?
If thou knewst what twere to be
Crown'd with that eternitie,
Which in all perfection flowes,
And nor end nor measure knowes,
Thou wouldst not such glorie loose.

Those

Those sweet Syrens, which do winne
  Sensual man to shame and sinne,
  Can their proper fortunes tell,
  If thou do but thinke on hell,
    Wh re the damned spirits dwell.
Sense may guesse, but cannot know
  Blisse diuine, infernal woe:
  They aboue conceipt are such,
  Good and ill; in each so much,
    That no thought their depth can touch.
Soules that from their bodies flie,
  (When they do dissolue and die)
  To celestial ioyes are flowne,
  Or to endlesse paines are throwne,
    But to whethet ti's vnknowne.
Mourning waites vpon the graue,
  That's the end we all must haue:
  Good and bad one death sustaine,
  But vnequal lotts retaine,
    Of eternal ioy or paine.
Flesh and blood once wrapt in lead,
  (Though the hearse be honoured)
  Teares, and triumphes nought auaile;
  Soules imprison'd find no baile,
    If their worth and merit faile.
Time out runnes the time to pray,
  Flight findes neither place nor way;
  Hope and feare are then too late,

                                    Sad

Sad repentance out of date,
 If we enter once the gate.
Wilt thou vpward, thou must stoope;
 Wilt thou downward, thou shalt vp:
 Humble hearts exalted flie,
 Whiles the proud deiected lie,
  In a world of miserie.
Soules polluted, though they rise,
 Share no part in this rich prize:
 If they haue from IESVS sweru'd,
 Or his mother slightly seru'd,
  Or no patron els deseru'd.
Who before a Iudge so strict
 Dares to pleade for one conuict?
 Those bright Angells that attend,
 Will their teares in pittie spend,
  Yet the righteous Iudge commend.
When the sentence once is past
 On the guiltie soule disgrast,
 Heau'nly powers with mutual ayde
 Scorne, contemne, reiect, vpbraid
  Her; that pleades, shee was betraid.
Then from those her proper facts
 Shee her proper guilt extracts:
 And condemnes her foolish trust,
 Vainely fixt on clay and dust,
  Yeelding yet her Iudge is iust.
Horrid shapes, and ouglie sightes,

Xx

Monsters

Monsters, fiendes, and mishapt sprites,
Raging torments, cruel smart,
Seize, and teare her in each part,
    Whiles shee feeles but her desert.
Eares, and tongues (not deafe, not dumbe)
Heare aud speake, yet cannot summe :
Euerie sense falles short, that would
By exteriour signes vnfold,
    What shee feeles, being there enrol'd.
Wonders that appeare most strange
Sense may to amazement change :
Yet the passion being past,
Reason giues a truer tast
    Of the obiect her disgrast.
But these curst infernal stormes
Wander in so many formes,
(Still successiue) that they are
Numberlesse without compare,
    Such as no man can declare.
Stormie cold, and raging heate,
Cloid, yet neuer full of meate,
Endlesse labour, fruitlesse toyle,
Scalding sulphur quencht with oyle,
    These these wretched soules embroyle.
Egresse thence no eie can finde,
    Where the flames still scortch the blinde :
Burning darknes, where they stand
Drownd in waters, though on land,
                Chaos

Chaos with confusion man'd.
As these are beyond beliefe,
  Great and strange in sense and griefe:
  So is that same blessed state
  Of saluation, without date,
    More then can the tongue relate.
When in glorie face to face
  We, in perfect ioy and grace,
  Shall behold that purest light,
  Without shadow, clowd, or night,
    In a world of all delight.
Honour then with triumph brings
  Vs, before the King of kings;
  Where a quire of Angells sound
  Noates in sweetnes, that abound,
    Whiles we sit in glorie crown'd.
If we might our wishes haue,
  We can neither wish nor craue,
  What we heere in fulnes finde,
  To each sense in euerie kinde,
    Farre aboue our thoughtes assign'd.
Free from care and all distresse,
  In a world of happines,
  Not for minutes, dayes, or yeares,
  Not for time that wastes and weares,
    But for euer, without feares.
Neuer eare by heare-say learn'd,
  Nor hath mortal eie discern'd:

Xx 2   Thought

Thought it selfe in his best way
Cannot thinke, see, heare, or say
   The least passage of this ioy.
Since we then in part may see,
   What those diuerse fortunes be,
   That both good and bad attend,
   When this mortal life doth end,
   Why in time do we not mend?
Tis not safe, that fond delay
   Do the season steale away:
   If we seize the time and place,
   Teares repentant sinnes deface,
   And do fitlie pleade for grace.
Death o're takes vs wretched men,
   If we liue as beastes: yet then
   We must feele what they not know,
   Good or ill, in ioy or woe,
   As we make our reck'ning goe.
Let vs then for pardon sue,
   And our prayers still renew:
   He that doth for mercie pleade
   From so mild a Iudge, may speed,
   Where so many interceade.
All things to confusion runne;
   Goodnes liues, but yet vndonne:
   All the world consumes away,
   Vertues beautie doth decay,
   And decreaseth euerie day.

If

If we hope for to aspire,
  We must maister our desire :
  And with winged spirits soare
  To the throne that can restore
    Dead men, if they life implore.
Call on him, whose gratious eare,
  When thou pray'st, enclines to heare:
  He that for vs sinners died,
  Must be seru'd, obey'd, and ei'd,
    Honour'd, lou'd, and magnified.
      AMEN.

OTHER

OTHER DEVOVT Verses, shevving the seueritie of the last general iudgement: and therfore crauing mercie novv before hand.

AT that day, that fearefull day,
    Day of iudgement, day of anger:
    When the guiltie soule must pay
    Tribute to eternal danger.
As the Prophet Dauid saieth,
  And Sibylla hath foretold vs;
  Fire, the messenger of wrath,
  Shall on euerie side enfold vs.
Then the world in flames shall burne,
  Liuing creatures then shall perish:
  All shall to confusion ruine,
  That the earth or ayre doth cherish.

                              Feare

Feare and trembling shall possesse
  Euerie liuing soule with terrour;
  When the glorious Iudge shall presse
  To each one his proper errour.
Vaultes, and graues, and hollow ground
  Shall their closed brimmes vncouer:
  When the trumpet shrill doth sound,
  They their prisoners must discouer.
Death his summons forth will send,
  To giue warning to each creature;
  That there then must be an end
  Of the world, of time, and nature.
All the dead must then appeare,
  When the Iudge shall sit in iudgement:
  And the fatal sentence heare,
  Which discourseth their engagement.
That black booke, that doth containe
  All our faultes, shall be produced:
  To excuse tis then in vaine,
  Or to pleade, we were seduced.
What (alas) can I enforce,
  When the iust are not secured,
  If that iustice haue his course,
  Which way can I be assured?
To what patron can I flie,
  That may be mine intercessor:
  When my sinnes vncouered lie,

And

And I am mine owne confessor?
Gratious God, great King of kings,
  For thy tender mercie saue me,
  Shade me vnderneath thy wings,
  Let not mine owne guilt depraue me.
Thou that art that glorious sonne,
  Who becam'ft the world's Redeemer:
  My poore soule will be vndonne,
  If that thou do difefteeme her.
Since thy sufferings on the crofse,
  Full of griefe, and bitter anguifh,
  Was to expiate my lofse;
  Do not fuffer me to languish.
Thou which art all goodnes pure,
  Full of gentle sweet compaffion:
  Let not me the ftormes endure
  Of fo sad an alteration.
Let not that thy pretious blood,
  Spent fo freelie for my ranfome,
  Be in vaine, but doe me good;
  For to cleanfe and make me handfome.
Thou great glorious Iudge behold
  With a gratious eie my forrow,
  That doth his owne teares enfold,
  And doth not from others borrow.
Blushes on my withered cheekes,
  Their owne proper guilt difplaying;

              From

From thy mercie, mercie seekes,
  Their desert themselues gaine-saying.
Let my mourning pearce thine eare,
  That heard Marie's dolefull crying;
  And releeu'd the theefe from feare,
  In the minute he was dying.
My poore prayers clad in truth,
  Pleade repentance in submission;
  And those errors of my youth,
  Prostrate with a true contrition
In thy flock giue me a place
  On thy right hand: If thou call me
  I shall neuer taste disgrace;
  Sinne and shame cannot forestall me.
Number me (sweet Father) there,
  Where thou dost enroll the blessed:
  That I may with comfort heare,
  Come you Soules, that are distressed,
Humbly on my bended knee,
  With a contrite heart I render
  This poore sacrifice to thee,
  Gratiouslie accept my tender.
When that day of teares an griefe
  Shall surprize the world with wonder:
  Tis too late to seeke reliefe,
  If thou do thy vengeance thunder.

Y y

Thou beſt Interceſſor pleade
  My ſweet Sauiour by thy merit :
  Let thy paſſion interceade,
  We ſaluation may inherit.

AMEN.

FINIS.

The

THE TABLE OF
the third Mirrour.

FINIS.